Battlefield Tour Guide of Bedford County Soldiers at Gettysburg & Antietam

Kevin Mearkle

Cover: Library of Congress photograph of Confederate soldiers near the Dunker Church taken shortly after the battle of Antietam.

The authors previous book was dedicated
to the Civil War Soldiers of Bedford County
who gave their lives for our country.

*Battlefield Tour Guide of
Bedford County Soldiers at
Gettysburg & Antietam*

*is dedicated to three Bedford County citizen soldiers ...
Jonathan S. Foor
Francis W. Pee
William W. VanOrmer
who were battlefield casualties during both Confederate
invasion attempts of Pennsylvania.*

Battlefield Tour Guide of Bedford County Soldiers at Gettysburg & Antietam

First Edition

Copyright © 2022 Kevin Mearkle

All rights reserved. No portion of this book may be reproduced in any form without permission from the author, except as permitted by U.S. copyright law.

For permissions contact: kevinmearklehistory@gmail.com

Contents

Introduction	*vii*
1. *Antietam Campaign*	*1*
2. *South Mountain*	*3*
3. *Antietam*	*13*
4. *Harpers Ferry*	*40*
5. *Gettysburg*	*48*
Notes	*74*

The sites where our citizen soldiers fought and died are not always well marked or easy to locate. Step by step driving directions are provided in larger print with approximate odometer milage distances to assist with locating the sites referenced. All Civil War era battlefield photographs are courtesy of the Library of Congress. Other photographs are courtesy of the author unless otherwise noted. Casualty listings compiled by the author. Battlefield maps are color-coded in numerical order of the movements of regiments that suffered multiple Bedford County casualties during each battle.

An unknown color bearer holds the remnants of the 8th Pennsylvania Reserves battle flag. During the Civil War, it was considered an honor to be a color bearer and guide fellow soldiers on the confusing and smoke-filled battlefields of the war. Because of the practical and symbolic importance of battle flags, a color bearer was an immediate primary target of enemy rifle fire, and their casualty rates were extraordinarily high. It was not unusual for multiple color-bearers in a unit being killed or wounded during a single battle.

Introduction

Few places in America are blessed with a local history equal to Bedford County. Part of this rich heritage is an enduring gift of firsthand documentation on what was witnessed on Civil War battlefields, some of which are contained on the following pages.

The Civil War differed from other military conflicts in our history in three ways.

Had the Union Army not prevailed, slavery would not have ended in 1865, and America likely would have been divided into separate countries... forever. The stakes could not have been much higher.

Many Bedford County families paid a terrible price for our country and freedom. The Civil War Soldiers of Bedford County book listed 585 Soldiers who lost their lives from 1861 to 1866. In the year since this book was published, an additional 17 men and boys have been identified. From a historical perspective, more soldiers from Bedford County perished during the handful of years of the Civil War than in all other wars from the French and Indian War through the recent war in Afghanistan... combined.

The Civil War did not take place on distant battlefields in Europe, the Middle East, or Southeast Asia. Our citizen soldiers fought and died in our own backyard. The Bedford Gazette reported cannon fire was heard in the county during the battle of 1st Bull Run, which is near today's Dulles Airport. During the war, many battles were fought in much closer proximity to Bedford County. Therefore, families living on properties we now call home would have often been reminded of their loved ones being in harm's way during the war.

Research is being done for a follow-up book to the "Civil War Soldiers of Bedford County." The title of this book will be "Walking in Footsteps" and subtitled "A story of the courage and sacrifices of Bedford County's Civil War Generation." The "Walking in Footsteps" book will cover the story part of the Civil War from the perspective of soldiers on the war front and their families back home.

After reading testimonies of those who were there and walking where they walked; return visits to Gettysburg and the battlefields of the Antietam campaign revealed a new, more meaningful dimension to the ground I was standing on. This led to a recent decision to write this book on two of the most consequential military campaigns in American history which were fought within close driving distance of Bedford County.

Robert E. Lee made two invasion attempts of Pennsylvania hoping to win a decisive victory on northern soil and force Abraham Lincoln to end the costly war he was waging. During the first Confederate invasion, Bedford County soldiers fought on the steepest terrain of any battle during the Civil War at South Mountain, were part of a garrison that defended Harper's Ferry, and were key combatants in turning back the Rebel army on the rolling hills surrounding the town of Sharpsburg near Hagerstown. Soon after the battle, Antietam became recognized as one of the most transformational events in American history when Abraham Lincoln pulled out a previously penned document from his desk. The Emancipation Proclamation freed all slaves in the Confederate states if the Union Army prevailed in the war. Lincoln had been waiting for a significant battlefield success to issue the order, so it would not appear to be an act of wartime desperation.

A short distance down the road on the Lincoln highway, a second Rebel Army invasion culminated in the most famous battle ever fought in the Western Hemisphere. Lee was turned away at Gettysburg, which may have been the Confederacy's last best chance to force an end to the war and succeed from the United States. Four months later, Lincoln traveled by train to Gettysburg for the dedication of a cemetery for those who died in the battle and delivered some of the most memorable prose in American history.

This book is solely focused on the regiments that suffered Bedford County casualties. Information on other Union Army regiments in close battlefield proximity are omitted. Civil War soldiers were often in life and death struggles against a determined enemy. A surprising number of firsthand details can be found in regimental histories, memoirs, letters and official army records. This book provides brief visceral glimpses of what Bedford County soldiers experienced from these primary source materials.

Antietam Campaign Map

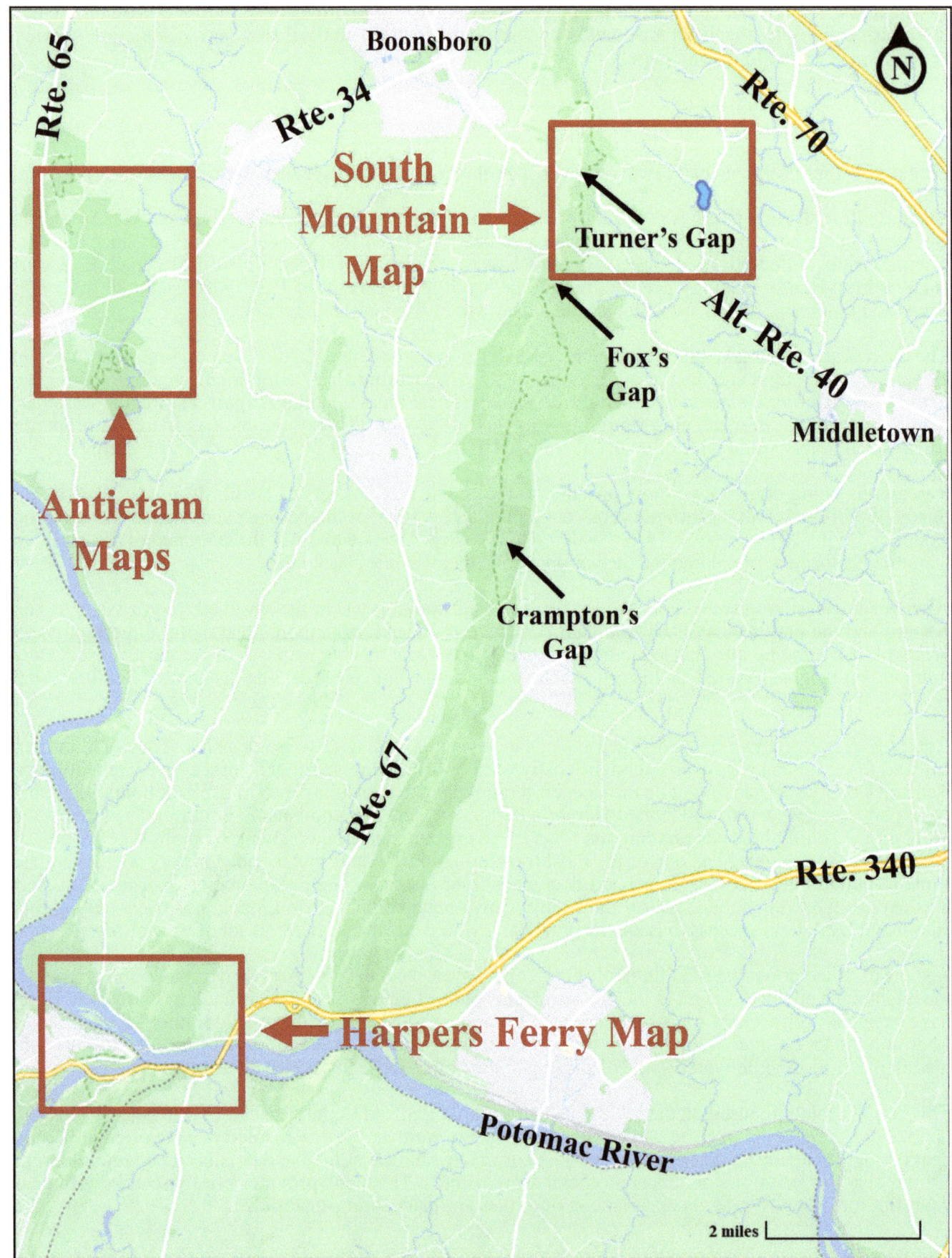

Antietam Campaign Overview

The Confederate forces of Robert E Lee routed the Union army at the 2nd battle of Bull Run near Manassas Junction, Virginia on August 30th, 1862. Lee sensed an opportunity and made immediate plans to invade Pennsylvania. On September 6th, the Confederate army marched into Frederick, MD and received a cool, mostly unsympathetic reception from the populace.[1] The following are some observations of the Rebel army from a citizen who remained in Frederick during the occupation, "I have never seen a mass of such filthy strong-smelling men. Three in a room would make it unbearable, and when marching in a column along the street, the smell from them was most offensive. The filth that pervades them is most remarkable. They have no uniforms, but are all well-armed and equipped, and have become so inured to hardships that they care but little for any of the comforts of civilization. These are the roughest looking set of creatures I ever saw, their features, hair and clothing matted with dirt and filth, and the scratching they kept up gave a warrant of vermin in abundance." [2]

While in Frederick, Maryland, Lee made a fateful decision to divide his army. 11,000 Union soldiers were garrisoned at Harpers Ferry and another 2500 troops were in Martinsburg, WV.[3] If Lee allowed these soldiers to remain at his rear, his communications and supply lines would be in jeopardy during the invasion. On September 9th, Lee issued Special Order #191 dispatching Stonewall Jackson to force the surrender of the garrison at Harpers Ferry and to clear out the remaining Union troops in Martinsburg before quickly reuniting with Lee's main army group near Boonsboro on the west side of South Mountain.

Lee did not expect the ever-cautious commanding general of the Union Army, George McClellan, would launch an attack on his divided army. After the Confederate army vacated Frederick, a Union army soldier found a lost copy of Special Order #191 in a meadow near the town. The Confederate invasion plans were quickly passed up the chain of command. McClellan, realizing Lee's divided army was vulnerable, launched an attack on three passes at South Mountain on September 14th. If the Union Army punched through Crampton's Gap, Fox's Gap or Turner's Gap, McClellan could launch an attack on Lee's divided army and possibly cutoff Stonewall Jackson from reuniting with Lee.[4]

Abraham Lincoln made a "vow" to God during the invasion. If the Rebel army was driven back from Pennsylvania, he would make a declaration of freedom to the slaves.[5] The following is the story of the Bedford County citizen soldiers who drove the Confederate Army troops off South Mountain, were participants in the deadliest day in American military history at Antietam and whose determined efforts to avoid capture at Harpers Ferry delayed Stonewall Jackson's troops from reuniting with Lee's main army group.

Photograph of Confederate Troops marching out of Frederick, MD

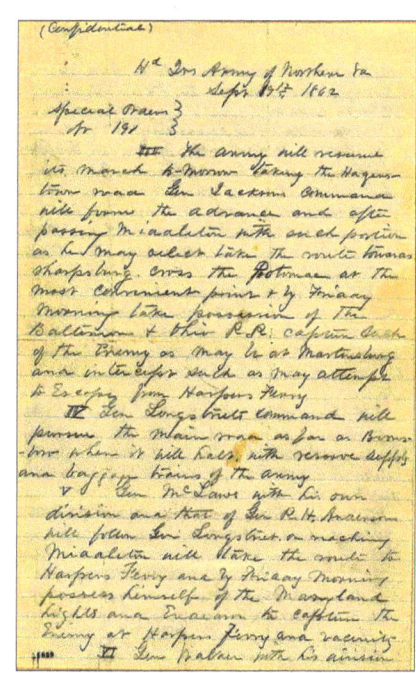

Copy of Special Order #191

South Mountain - known Bedford Co. casualty listing

Name	Muster Age	Rank	State	Regiment	Company	Casualty
Eidenbaugh, John	37	Pvt.	PA	107th Infantry	H	Wounded
Figart, Levi H	17	Pvt.	PA	107th Infantry	H	Wounded
Foor, Jonathan S	22	Pvt.	PA	107th Infantry	H	Wounded
Gates, George W	18	Pvt.	PA	13th Reserves	D	Wounded
Horton, George	21	Corp.	PA	8th Reserves	F	Wounded
Kay, William H	20	Corp.	PA	8th Reserves	F	Wound.-Died
Mellott, Frederick	21	Pvt.	PA	12th Reserves	K	KIA
Riley, Andrew J	16	Pvt.	PA	107th Infantry	H	Wounded
Shaw, Matthew P	22	Pvt.	PA	8th Reserves	F	KIA

Andrew J Foor was 31 years old when he left his East Providence Township home to muster in the 107th PA Infantry in March 1862. He survived the war and passed at the age of 78. Andrew is buried at the Rays Cove Christian Cemetery.[1]

Drawing of Union Soldiers charging Confederates holding the higher ground at Turner's Gap during the Battle of South Mountain. There are no known Civil War era photographs of the Turner's Gap battlefield.[2]

8th PA Reserves, Hopewell Rifles Company Officers

Eli Eichelberger was born in Hopewell in 1840. He mustered in the Hopewell Rifles Company of the 8th PA Reserves as a 1st Lieutenant in June 1861. Eli later suffered a wound in the left thigh on May 6th, 1864, during the battle of the Wilderness. He recovered from his wound and returned home to Bedford County. Eli married Helen Wishart in 1866 and was a father to two sons. He was the proprietor of the E. Eichelberger and Son store in Saxton. Eli passed at age 75 on May 18th, 1915 and is buried in the Everett Cemetery.[3]

Lewis B Waltz was born around 1827. Lewis was mustered as a 2nd lieutenant in the Hopewell Rifles Company of the 8th PA Reserves in June 1861. He received a promotion to captain on October 30, 1863. Lewis mustered out with the rest of his regiment on May 26th, 1864. He returned to Bedford County and married Margaret Long in August 1864. Lewis passed on June 26th, 1881 and is buried in the Saint Luke's Cemetery in Saxton.[4]

Soldiers in the Hopewell Rifles Company pose in front of a Virginia residence in 1861. Eli Eichelberger is the only identified soldier. He is standing behind a chair with his arms folded.[5]

At Breezewood take I-70 East & proceed 65 miles to exit 42 MD-17 South.

Take MD-17 South & proceed 5.2 miles.

Right on Alt. US-40 & proceed 3.0 miles.
Once you turn on Alt. US-40, also known as the Old National Pike, you will be traveling on the same roads as Bedford County soldiers marched on to the Turner's Gap battlefield.

Right on Mt. Tabor Rd. & proceed 1.0 mile.
Once you reach the Station Rd. / Mt. Tabor Rd. intersection, on the right will be the site of the Mt. Tabor Church. The 8th PA Reserves turned off Mt. Tabor Rd. near the church and formed a battle line for the assault on Turner's Gap. Please note there are no Civil War markers on the Turner's Gap battlefield you will be touring.

The Mt. Tabor Church stood close to the red outbuilding in the above photograph.

Photograph of the Mt. Tabor Church taken in 1922 prior to being dismantled.

Turner's Gap map - September 14th, 1862

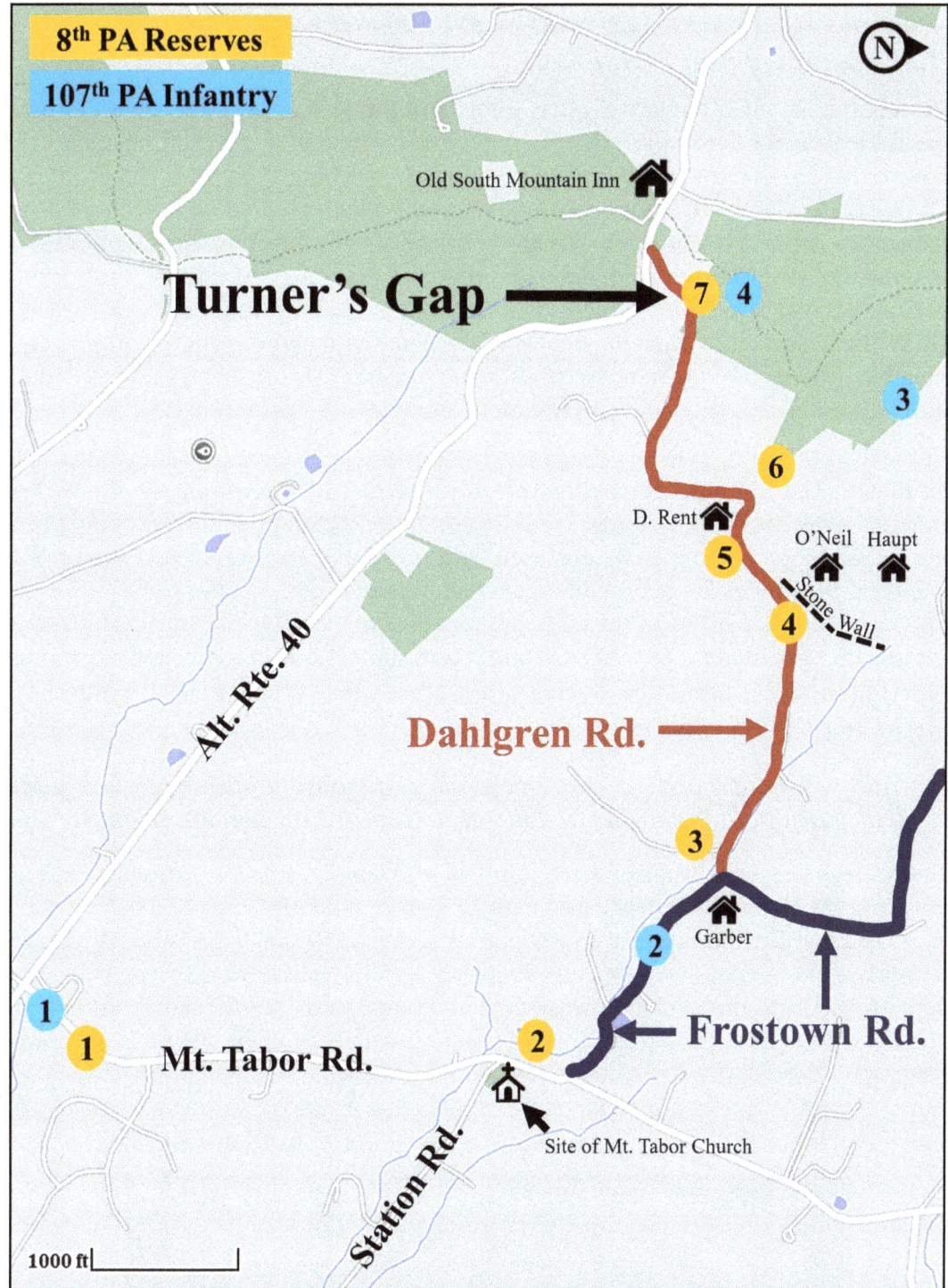

Please note Frederick Mellott of the 12th PA Reserves was killed during the Turner's Gap assault and would have been positioned 1000 to 1500 feet to the right of the 8th PA Reserves during the charge up South Mountain. George W. Gates of the 13th PA Reserves was wounded during the battle and would have been positioned 2000 to 3000 feet to the right of the 8th PA Reserves.

There are no Civil War markers on this section of the Turner's Gap battlefield. Locations of landmark structures that existed during the battle are included on the above map and photographs are provided of these structures on the following pages.

Proceed 0.1 miles & take a left at the Frostown Rd.

Please reset your automobile odometer to zero. Milage distances will be periodically provided from the Mt. Tabor Rd / Frostown Rd. intersection during the accent to the Turner's Gap summit of South Mountain.

On September 14th, 1862, Bedford County soldiers in the 1st Corps of the Union Army gathered for their usual breakfast of hardtack and coffee prior to the start of a march from their camp along the Monocacy river. Union soldiers received an enthusiastic welcome from the townspeople as they passed through Frederick, Maryland, around 8:00 am. Veteran William Henry Locke wrote a history of the 11th PA Regiment in 1868. In the book, he stated, "It was a Sabbath morning, clear and beautiful, when the Federal army marched through Frederick - an event always to be remembered. For one week, the town had been under rebel rule, a time sufficiently long for even the most intense Southern sympathizer; and the sight of the Union ranks filled the people of the place with extravagant joy. Amid deafening cheers and flying banners and waving handkerchiefs, we pressed our way through the crowded streets toward the South Mountain, that rose boldly in front to the height of a thousand feet." [6]

By the time the Pennsylvania Reserve regiments, commanded by General George Meade, began the assault on Turner's Gap around 4:00, they had already marched 17 miles along Alt. Rte. 40 from Frederick before reaching the Mt. Tabor Church. Frank Holsinger of the Hopewell Rifles company of the 8th PA Reserves recalled, "At the church we deployed, and no sooner had we formed than a few shots came whizzing from the mountain, but double-quicking, we soon passed out of sight of the rebel battery." [7] In an 1864 memoir, Ashbel Hill of the 8th PA Reserves wrote, "a rebel battery was posted at the summit of the mountain opened upon us with shell and round shot. We soon succeeded in gaining the cover of an abrupt ridge near the base of the mountain. The battery then ceased to play. A line of battle was now formed, and preparations were made to move forward." [8]

Proceed 0.5 miles & take a left on Dahlgren Rd. Please note Dahlgren is a public road, but all the cited battlefield locations at Turner's Gap are on private property.

The 8th PA Reserves were on the extreme left flank of George Meade's battle line during the battle of Turner's Gap. The Hopewell Rifles rushed past the Garber farmhouse pictured below[9] and advanced on the left of Dahlgren Rd. through a steep wooded area. Frank Holsinger described the terrain at Turner's Gap as "broken into deep gulley's or gorges running parallel; and as we advanced, the country became still more broken until the mountain was reached. So irregular was the terrain that to keep anything like a line was next to impossible. Here there were great rocks to be scaled by pushing and pulling each other up or making detours around impenetrable patches of briars that everywhere covered those mountains. The advance was ordered to attack, but so dense was the forest and so irregular the surface of the country that the line could not be seen on either side 100 yards distant." [10]

Proceed to the O'Neal House shown in the photo below (1.0 mile on odometer).

The 12th Alabama infantry was positioned behind a stone wall one mile up from Mt. Tabor Rd./ Frostown Rd. intersection near the O'Neil farmhouse. Ashbell Hill of the 8th PA Reserves recalled, "A few hundred yards from the base of the mountain, was a stone-fence. Below this, the ground was clear; above, the face of the mountain was covered with trees and rocks. When within fifty yards of the stone-fence, a murderous fire of musketry was opened upon us by the rebels, who lay concealed behind it, and swarms of bullets whistled about our ears. With a wild shout, we dashed forward-almost upward-while volley after volley was poured upon us; but we heeded it not; we rushed madly on. The rebels, intimidated by our voices, and taken aback by our recklessness and disregard of their bullets, began to give way. We reached the stone-fence and sprang over. The rebels reformed among the rocks and fought with remarkable obstinacy." [11]

In a 1906 memoir, Confederate captain Robert Emory Park of the 12th Alabama infantry described the 8th PA Reserves assault at Turner's Gap, "I concealed my men behind trees, rocks and bushes, and cautioned them to aim well before firing. We awaited with bated breath and beating hearts, the sure and steady approach of Pennsylvania soldiers, who were in front of us, and soon near enough to fire upon. In response to my loud command, the men fired, almost simultaneously, and we drove back the skirmishers to their main line. The solid, well-drilled line advanced steadily forward. My men slowly fell back, firing from everything which screened them from observation. Several of them were wounded and six or eight became completely demoralized by the unbroken front of the rapidly approaching enemy, and despite my commands, entreaties, and threats they left me, and hastily fled to the rear. Brave Corporal Myers, of Mobile, adopting a suggestion of mine, aimed and fired at an exposed officer, receiving a mortal wound in the breast as he did so. I raised him tenderly, offered him water, and was rising to reluctantly abandon him to his fate when a dozen muskets were pointed at me, and I was ordered to surrender. There was a ravine to our left, and the 3rd Alabama skirmishers had fallen back. The Yankees had got to my rear, and closed upon me in front. If I had not gone to Myers when he fell, I might have escaped capture. I was mortified and humiliated by the necessity of yielding myself a prisoner. Certain death was the only alternative. One of the men, who ran away early in the action, reported that I had been killed, and my name was so published in the Richmond papers, and my relatives mourned me as one dead, until I was regularly exchanged and reached Richmond." [12]

The O'Neil house is on the left and the Haupt house on the right. Photo was taken 100 ft. past the 1900A Dahlgren Rd. address marker.   *Capt. Robert Emory Park 12th Alabama Infantry* [13]

The 8th PA Reserves continued to press the retreating Alabama soldiers up the steep terrain along both sides of Dahlgren Road. Holsinger recalled, "Our line had followed them up closely, and at the command to charge we rushed forward, driving them from their covert (concealed positions) and capturing some prisoners, besides killing and wounding many." [14] As the 8th Reserves were making their way up the mountain, the 17th South Carolina Infantry was descending from the Turner's Gap summit toward the D. Rent farmhouse.

Pause when you reach the clearing below the D. Rent House property as shown in the below photograph (1.2 miles on odometer).

Photograph of the D. Rent House on the right is partially obscured by trees. The 8th PA Reserves surprised the 17th South Carolina in the field on the left.

5 Around 6:00 the 17th South Carolina Infantry was moving through a small field 500 feet below the D. Rent farmhouse when they were surprised by the 8th PA Reserves. Ashbel Hill described the devastating volley, "We pressed the rebels closely. They stood awhile, loading and firing, but at last began to waver. Directly in front of the right of our regiment, they gave way; and several of our companies became detached from our regiment. We soon found ourselves thirty or forty paces ahead of the regiment, having gained the flank of the 17th South Carolina. We were within twenty or thirty steps of them, directly on their left, and they did not see us; then we mowed them down. Poor fellows! I almost pitied them, to see them sink down by dozens at every discharge!" [15] The 17th South Carolina retreated, formed a new line of battle about 300 yards up the mountain, where they were flanked a second time by the PA Reserves, and forced to retire on the other side of Turner's Gap. Col. F.W. McMaster of the 17th Carolina wrote of their heavy losses in his official report. 61 South Carolina soldiers were killed, missing or wounded out of 141 who took part in the battle.[16]

Proceed to Turner's Gap summit (1.5 miles on Odometer).
The 8th PA Reserves advanced across Dahlgren Rd. where the road veers around the D. Rent House.

Photograph taken from above the D. Rent House on Dahlgren Road.

The 8th PA Reserves crossed Dahlgren Road near the D. Rent House and continued to press the retreating Confederates. The 107th PA Infantry, which had been held in reserve, received orders to reinforce the PA Reserve regiments who were running low on ammunition. In his official report, Capt. James MacThomson of the 107th PA Infantry wrote, "at about 5:30 pm, we found the enemy fiercely engaged with the Pennsylvania Reserves. Immediately, in compliance with orders from General Duryea, we formed a battle line near the foot of the hill and gave orders to move forward with fixed bayonets. Nothing could exceed the promptness of both officers and men in the execution of this order; with enthusiastic cheers, they dashed forward, and soon the enemy were scattered, and in much confusion were flying before us. Several times they rallied, and once in particular, having gained an admirable position behind a stone fence, they appeared determined to hold on to the last. It was here they sustained their greatest loss. Colonel Gayle, 12th Alabama, fell dead, and a lieutenant-colonel of the 5th South Carolina was wounded and taken prisoner. Their stand did not delay the onward movement of the 107th and in a little while we were over the fence and among them, taking 68 prisoners, killing and wounding quite a number, and causing the remainder to fly precipitately to the top of the mountain. Following, we drove them across the narrow plain on the summit and part way down the other side. Night ended the pursuit; but, fearing a surprise, I directed officers and men to rest during the night, prepared for any emergency, and threw 200 yards in advance a volunteer picket of 10 men." [17]

(left) Jonathan S Foor was born on December 20th, 1839, in East Providence Township. He was 22 years old when he mustered in the 107th Pennsylvania Infantry on January 9th, 1862. His wife gave birth to their third child 9 days later. Jonathan suffered a wound on September 14th, 1862 at South Mountain. The following year, he was captured during the 1st day of the Battle of Gettysburg. Jonathan spent the next 17 months in several Confederate POW camps, including Andersonville, before being released on December 11th, 1864. Jonathan was a father to 10 children. He passed at age 68 and is buried in the Rays Cove Christian Church Cemetery outside of Breezewood.[18]

Col. Albert Magilton, commanding officer of the 8th PA Reserves, provided the following observations in his official report, "we advanced steadily to the front, driving the enemy over the mountain. Becoming quite dark, and our ammunition giving out, I took up a position and remained sleeping on our arms for the night. I have the pleasure to state that all did their duty well, and pushed forward with great courage, for which they deserve the highest praise." [19] A book on the "History of the Pennsylvania Reserve Corps" written in 1865 stated the 8th PA Reserves encountered a stronger force of the enemy, fought its way at every step, and sustained a heavier loss than all the other regiments of the Brigade combined at South Mountain.[20] But on that day, the 107th PA Regiment suffered the most Bedford County casualties during the last assault that drove the Confederates off Turner's Gap.

Many dead and wounded Confederates were lying among the rocks below the Turner's Gap summit. Captain Conner of the 8th PA Reserves approached one of the Confederate officers, who had suffered a severe thigh wound and appeared to be in intense pain. The following was their conversation according to Ashbel Hill, "You are wounded, are you not? Yes, in the thigh and badly. May I inquire your name? I am Major Means, of the 17th South Carolina. May I ask you the same question? I am Captain Conner, of the 8th Pennsylvania Reserves. Means replied, The - the - Pennsylvania Reserves. Well, captain, your men fight like devils; driving our men right up this steep mountain; I never could have believed it! Conner commented, ah, major, there is blood in Pennsylvania as well as in South Carolina. Means replied, I am convinced of that." [21]

South Mountain

The stunning Union army victory at the battle of South Mountain stopped the first rebel invasion of Pennsylvania in its tracks and set up the epic battle of Antietam three days later. This battle was over, but for some families in Bedford County, the mourning of a loved one was just beginning.

William H. Kay mustered in the Hopewell Rifles Company of the 8th PA Reserves in June 1861. He was struck in the abdomen by minie ball below Turner's Gap. William died 4 days later on September 18th. After William died, his father Isaac drove to Maryland in a family farm wagon to locate his son's body. His father packed the body in salt and brought William home for burial in St. Paul's Cemetery in Yellow Creek. On the left is his gravestone. William was a couple months shy of his 22nd birthday. William also left behind 7 younger siblings. Below is a copy of a pension request made by his mother 3 years prior to her death in 1892.[22]

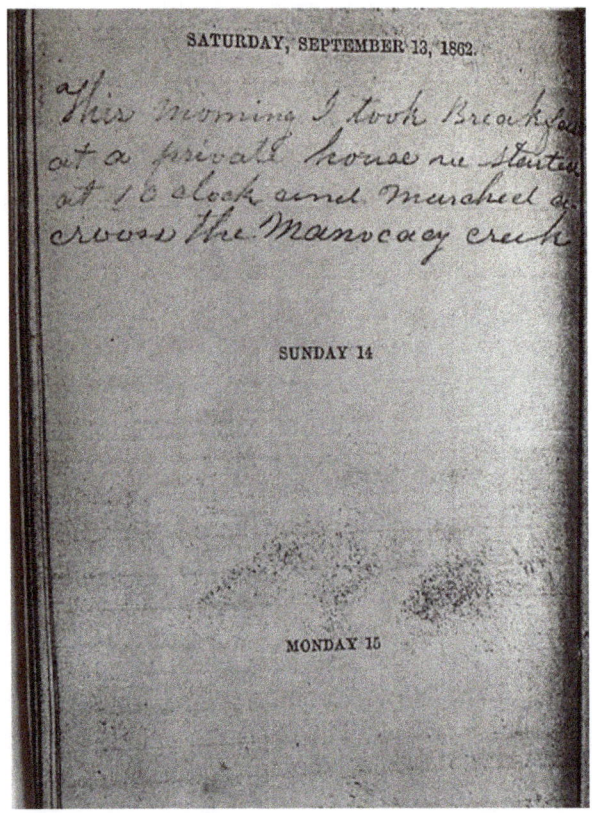

Matthew P. Shaw volunteered in the Hopewell Rifles company of the 8th PA Reserves on June 19th, 1861. Matthew carried a diary with him when he was killed during the assault on Turner's Gap on Sunday, September 14th, 1862. On the left is the diary entry on Saturday, September 13th, the day before he was killed. He wrote, "This morning I took breakfast at a private home. We started at 10 o'clock and marched across the Monocacy Creek."

Matthew was born in 1838 in Monroe Township. His parents, Benjamin and Susanna Mearkle Shaw, raised a large family of 7 daughters and 2 sons on their family farm. His enlistment documents stated he was 22 years old, 6'1" tall, with light hair, blue eyes and was a farmer.

The gravesite of Matthew P. Shaw is not known. There is a possibility he is lying in an unmarked grave at the Antietam National Cemetery.[23]

The following directions to the Antietam National Battlefield are via the same route taken by most Bedford County soldiers who took part in the battle of South Mountain.

From the Turner's Gap summit proceed 0.4 miles on Dahlgren Road down the western side of South Mountain until you reach Rte. 40 / Old National Pike.

Right on Rte. 40 / Old National Pike & proceed 2.5 miles to Boonsboro.

Left on Rte. 34 / Potomac Street and & proceed 3.5 miles.

Right on Keedysville Rd. & proceed 0.7 miles to the Hitt Bridge.

1862 photograph of the Hitt bridge crossed by most Bedford County soldiers in route to Antietam.

Proceed over the Hitt Bridge and take an immediate left on Mansfield Rd.

Proceed on Mansfield for 1.9 miles

Left on Smoketown Rd. & proceed for 0.6 miles
You will pass through the Cornfield & Dunker Church sectors of the Antietam battlefield on the way to the Antietam Visitors Center.

Left on Dunker Church Rd. & proceed 0.2 miles.

Left on the Antietam Visitor Center drive.

The battlefield tour directions will start at the Antietam Visitor Center.

Union soldiers standing by the new grave of a comrade on the Antietam Battlefield shortly after the battle. This site is near the Antietam Visitor Center.

Confederate dead laying just southwest of the Cornfield. Alexander Gardner took the period photographs on the following pages the day after the battle. The graphic images of dead soldiers laying on the Antietam battlefield shocked the American public and affected perceptions of a war which was already deeply unpopular with some in the North.

Antietam Battlefield Map

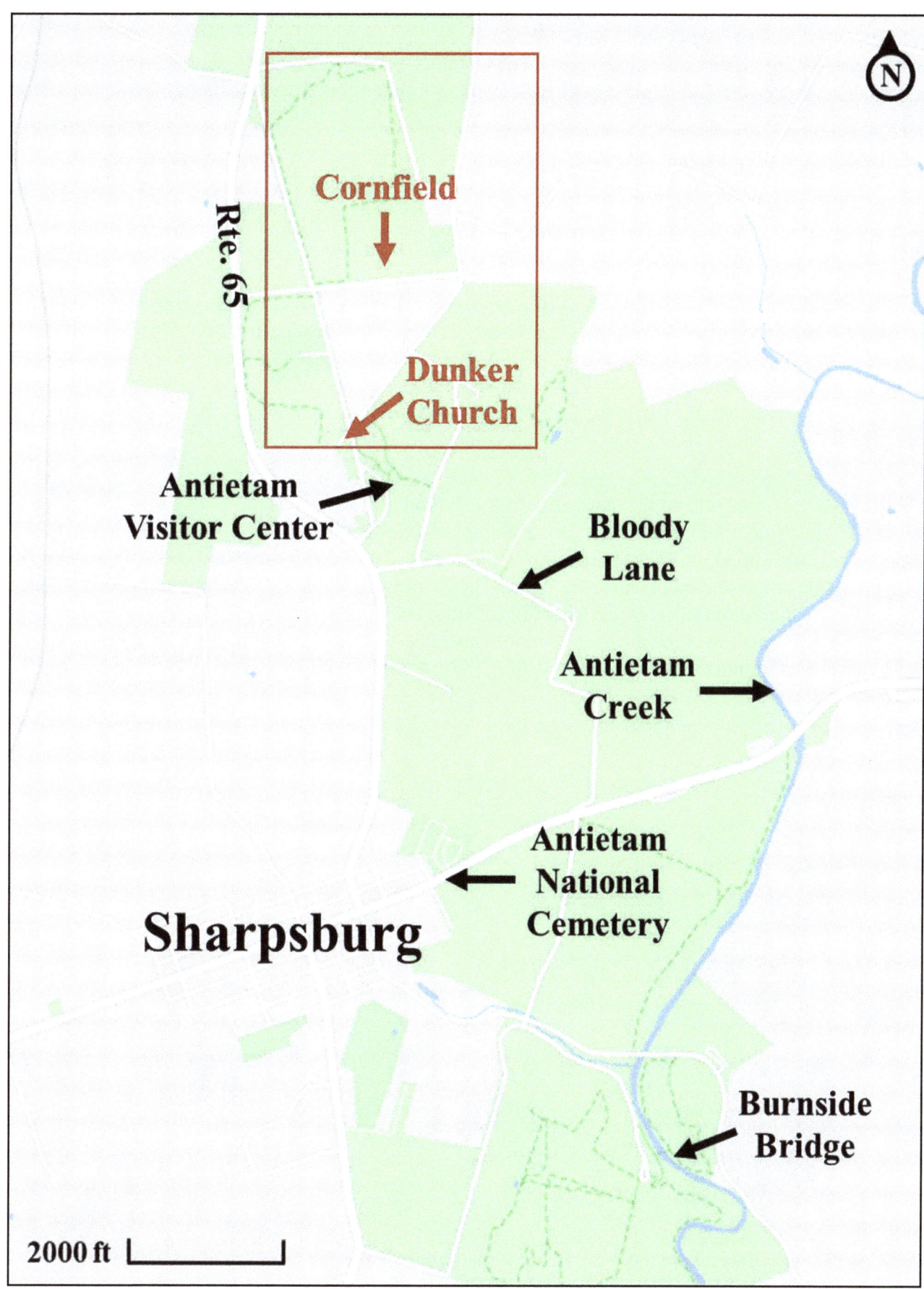

Antietam - September 17th, 1862

Cannon fire reverberated from a nearby ridge, interrupting a peaceful Sunday afternoon in the farmhouses near Antietam Creek on September 14th. Children in the Mumma family, who were playing outside, came running back into the house after observing plumes of smoke rising from South Mountain. The terrible civil war, which had been raging for over a year, had now come uncomfortably close to their home.[1]

Later that evening, the Union army won a significant victory when the Confederates were driven off the passes of South Mountain. Lee, realizing the perilous situation of his divided army, feverously completed plans to move his main army group from the western foothills of South Mountain to a more defensible position on the rolling hills across Antietam Creek, outside the town of Sharpsburg.

Commanding General of the Union Army, George McClellan, advanced cautiously from South Mountain. The first of 60,000 Union soldiers did not cross Antietam Creek until the afternoon on September 16th. That night, 14,000 Confederate troops arrived from Harpers Ferry, increasing Lee's forces to 35,000 men at Sharpsburg.[2] The bloodiest day in American military history began at first light on September 17th, 1862, when General Joseph Hooker advanced the Union Army First Corps across the Miller farm to a 20-acre Cornfield. The Cornfield area of the battlefield was the site of some of the most savage fighting of the Civil War. Around 9 am, Union soldiers drove the Confederates into the East Woods near the Dunker Church before being driven back.

By late morning, the heavy fighting shifted to the Sunken Road area of the battlefield. Later in the afternoon, the battle shifted a third time to the Burnside Bridge. Union troops were about to overtake the Confederate lines near the Burnside Bridge when the last of Stonewall Jackson's troops arrived from Harpers Ferry just in time to halt the Union advance. General McClellan failed to press an outnumbered Confederate Army during the battle and lost another chance to destroy Lee's army after the battle by allowing the Confederates to retreat across the Potomac River unmolested. Antietam ended in a tactical draw, with both sides suffering shockingly high casualties. Lincoln became more frustrated with McClellan in the weeks following Antietam when he failed to pursue the Rebel Army. McClellan was fired on November 7, 1862 and replaced with Ambrose Burnside.

Photograph of the burnt ruins of the Mumma farm the day after the battle.

Antietam - known Bedford County casualty listing

Name	Muster Age	Rank	State	Regiment	Company	Casualty
Baker, Franklin S	18	Pvt.	PA	125th Infantry	E	KIA
Black, George W Z	19	Capt.	PA	107th Infantry	H	Wounded
Bradley, James A	30	Pvt.	PA	8th Reserves	F	Wounded
Breneman, Michael B	24	Pvt.	PA	125th Infantry	C	Wounded
Bryant, James	25	Pvt.	PA	125th Infantry	F	Wounded
Burkholder, George		Pvt.	PA	125th Infantry	H	Wounded
Chaney, Levi	19	Pvt.	PA	107th Infantry	H	Wounded
Davis, James W	30	Pvt.	PA	28th Infantry	O	Wounded
Dean, Franklin		Pvt.	PA	8th Reserves	F	Wounded
Decker, Levi	23	Pvt.	PA	125th Infantry	H	Wounded
Dell, Moses	21	Pvt.	PA	1st Light Art.	F	Wounded
Fessler, Samuel		Pvt.	PA	107th Infantry	H	KIA
Foor, George W	43	Pvt.	PA	107th Infantry	H	KIA
Frazey, Frederick L	21	Pvt.	PA	11th Infantry	A	Wounded
Gaster, James H	18	Sgt.	PA	107th Infantry	H	Wound.-Died
Gates, James	23	Pvt.	PA	8th Reserves	F	Wound.-Died
Harclerode, David	20	Pvt.	PA	125th Infantry	E	Wounded
Horton, George	21	Corp.	PA	8th Reserves	F	Wound.-Died
Jamison, Benjamin	19	Pvt.	PA	125th Infantry	B	Wounded
Kelley, John A	23	Corp.	PA	125th Infantry	D	KIA
Lear, John	26	Pvt.	PA	125th Infantry	E	KIA
Leighty, John Q	23	Corp.	PA	8th Reserves	F	Wound.-Died
Malone, William	24	Pvt.	PA	8th Reserves	F	Wound.-Died
Maugle, Joseph	22	Pvt.	PA	8th Reserves	F	Wounded
Morse, David	16	Pvt.	PA	11th Infantry	A	Wound.-Died
Pee, Frances W	21	Sgt.	PA	11th Infantry	A	Wounded
Riley, William		Pvt.	PA	11th Infantry	A	Wound.-Died
Shorthill, David R	31	Pvt.	PA	125th Infantry	F	Wounded
Sigel, Stephen	36	Pvt.	PA	11th Infantry	A	Wounded
VanOrmer, William	20	Capt.	PA	53rd Infantry	I	Wounded
Weaverling, David	22	2nd Lt.	PA	11th Infantry	A	Wounded
Weaverling, Jacob P	33	Pvt.	PA	11th Infantry	A	KIA
White, Edmund H	25	Corp.	PA	8th Reserves	F	Wounded

There are 33 known Bedford County casualties during the battle of Antietam, including 13 soldiers who lost their lives. Thirty-two of the casualties took place in the Cornfield and Dunker Church areas of the battlefield during the morning hours of the battle. Captain William VanOrmer of the 53rd PA infantry was wounded during the Sunken Road assault in the middle of the day. The Cornfield and nearby areas accounted for about 6,500 of the 10,300 Confederate casualties and almost 7,300 of the 12,400 Union casualties during the battle of Antietam. The exact number of deaths at Antietam will never be known, but estimations are 3,650 Americans in the Union and Confederate Armies lost their lives on September 17th, 1862.[3] From a historical perspective, approximately 2,500 Americans lost their lives on D-Day during World War II.[4]

Cornfield sector battlefield map

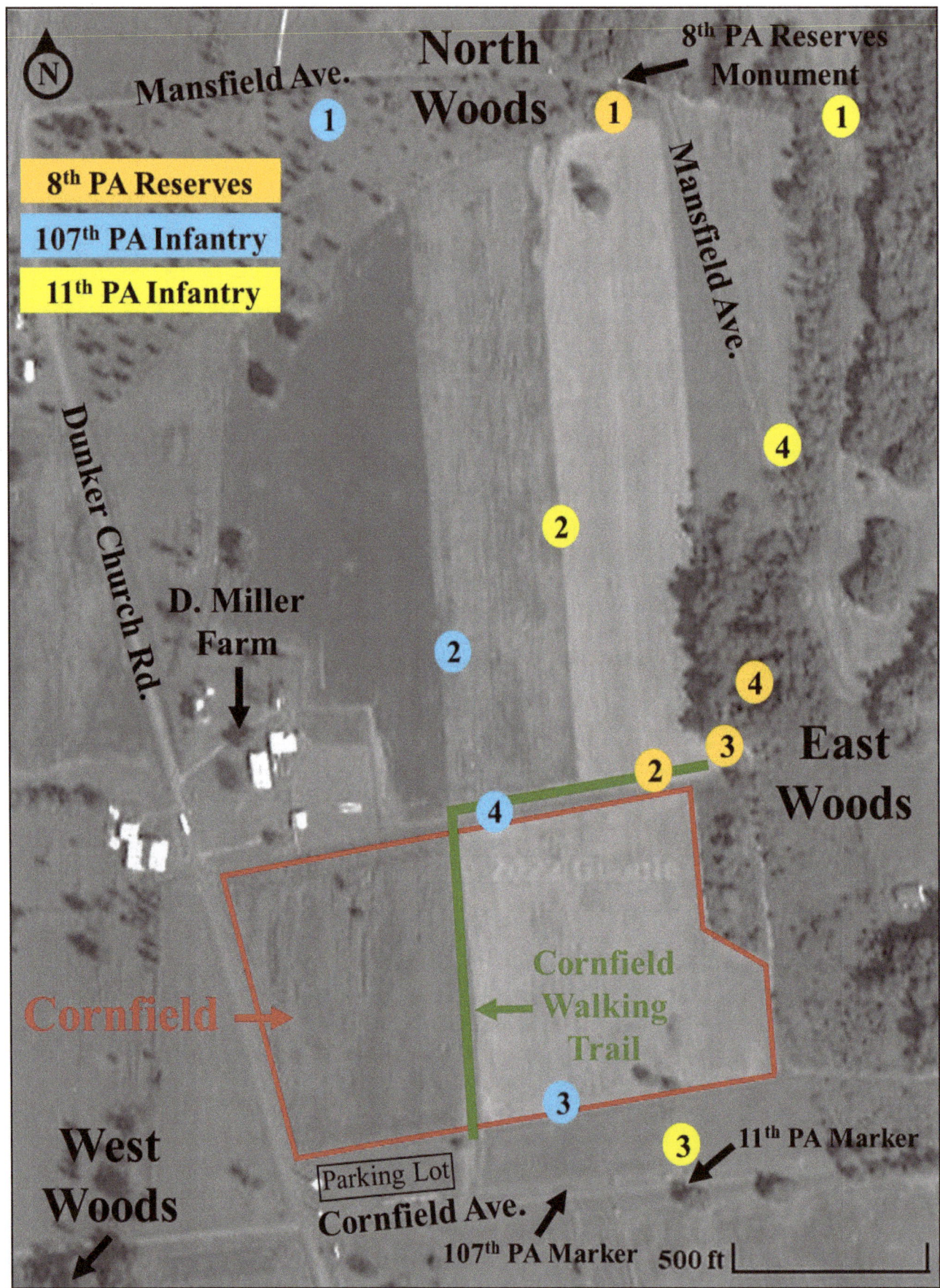

Frank Holsinger, pictured on the right, was one of nearly 100 Bedford County citizen soldiers who volunteered in the Hopewell Rifles Company of the 8th Pennsylvania Reserves during the summer of 1861. Frank was born and raised on a farm near Woodbury and was listed as a carpenter on the 1860 Middle Woodbury Township census. His 1861 enlistment record stated he was a 25-year-old teacher who stood 5'9" tall, had black hair, a dark complexion, and gray eyes.[5]

Frank survived four battlefield wounds during the Civil War. He was wounded at the battle of Fredericksburg 3 months after Antietam. In March 1864, he received a commission of captain in the newly formed 19th United States Color Troops (U.S.C.T.) infantry regiment. Holsinger suffered 3 wounds during the 2nd battle of Bermuda Hundred in November 1864. The first bullet struck his left forearm, a second minie ball slammed into his shoulder. Frank remained on the field before suffering a third wound that broke his right forearm and severed an artery. He survived the life-threatening wounds and mustered out of the army in January 1867, after his Union army unit served in the Freedmen's Bureau after the war ended.

Frank moved to Kansas City after the war and became a well-known horticulturist. He traveled to Washington, DC many times after the war to advocate for Civil War veteran's issues. The above photograph accompanied a newspaper article in August 1900 when Holsinger ran for governor of Kansas.[6]

Frank Holsinger wrote a letter on February 29, 1892, to John M. Gould, who was requesting testimony from veterans about what they experienced during the battle of Antietam. He provided much of the details of the following story of the Hopewell Rifles at Antietam.

Exit Antietam Visitors Center & take a Right on Dunker Church Rd. & proceed 0.9 miles.

Right on Mansfield Ave. & proceed 0.2 miles to the 8th Reserves Monument.

The Hopewell Rifles broke camp in an orchard on the west side of South Mountain at 2 pm, on September 16th, and advanced toward Sharpsburg. They crossed Antietam Creek at the Hitt Bridge and pressed forward while under rifle fire from skirmishing Confederates.

1 The 8th PA Reserves reached the wooded area just east of the J. Poffenberger Farm in the North Woods (across the road from where their monument on the right now stands) and began taking fire from a Confederate artillery battery on a knoll less than a quarter of a mile away. Brigadier General George Meade calmly walked to the front of

where the 8th PA Reserves were taking cover from the cannister shot, plunging into the trees above their heads. Meade stood near where Frank was hugging the ground and boldly asserted, "Oh but for two good regiments I'd take that damn battery. By two good regiments I mean 800 men. You are only 400." The 8th PA Reserves began the war with closer to a thousand men, but 15 months later, they were down to less than half strength because of battlefield casualties and disease. Frank was amazed Meade was so collected and apparently oblivious to the dangerous circumstance of Confederates shelling their position with shotgun type munitions.

Before first light the next morning, Meade returned to the exact spot and lamented, "Boys, we missed the golden opportunity of our lives. We could have taken that battery. It was supported by only a skirmish line," Holsinger believed a much larger contingent of Confederates supported the artillery battery. Then with a gesture and toss of his head, Meade proclaimed "our time will come soon, and we will have a chance to do something for Glory yet." Less than a year after the battle of Antietam, Abraham Lincoln unexpectedly placed Meade in charge of the Union Army of the Potomac in late June 1863 after Hooker resigned his post. Less than a week later, Meade was immortalized in history as the victorious commanding general at Gettysburg.

(left) George G. Meade was the Brigadier General of the PA Reserve regiments during the battles of South Mountain and Antietam. A brigadier is the lowest ranking general in the army. (right) The D. Miller family pictured on their porch two days after the battle. No close-up Civil War era photographs of the Cornfield on the Miller's property are known to exist.

At around 6:45 am, the 8th PA Reserves rushed on the double quick through the open fields of the D. R. Miller farm toward a sea of flames in and around the Cornfield. Once they reached the northern edge of the Cornfield, they feverishly began erecting a barricade out of the rail fencing when an order was shouted to rally to the East Woods, toward rebel soldiers who were taking deadly aim at Union artillerymen. The regiment rose and maneuvered less than 30 feet when a devastating volley was fired from the other side of the Cornfield rail fence by the 6th Georgia Infantry Regiment. Half of the soldiers near Frank Holsinger instantly dropped to the ground.

The three Hopewell Rifles soldiers standing closest to Frank were wounded. Edmund White was hit in the arm. Frank Dean fell to the ground behind him and on his left, James Gates was riddled by four minie balls. Holsinger and Gates were like brothers, and both promised should either be injured, they would look out for the other. Holsinger was standing between his best friend and the enemy when the horrific volley was fired and later wrote it was an eternal mystery about how he was unscathed, and Gates suffered four separate wounds.

Nearby George Horton, the color-bearer for the Hopewell Rifles, was on the ground with a shattered ankle from a minie ball. Any color-bearer became an immediate primary target of enemy fire because battle flags were the key to soldiers knowing the location of their units on the confusing, smoke-filled Civil War battlefields. Several soldiers begged George to hand them the battle flag, but George refused and answered, "Stay and defend them!" While on the ground, Horton held on to the battle flag and continued firing a revolver at the Confederates scrambling over the Cornfield rail fence. Seconds later, a Confederate soldier lowered his rifle and shot George Horton in the head. Lt. Lewis Waltz immediately stooped down, picked up a rifle and shot the rebel, who fell over the split-rail fence.[7]

Lt. Lewis Waltz of the Hopewell Rifles.[8]

Photograph taken in 1911 of Hopewell Rifles veterans. The man holding the flag on the far left is David Horton. There is little doubt David is paying homage to his brother George, who died at Antietam, while holding the Hopewell Rifles battle flag. Standing next to David Horton is Captain Eli Eichelberger.[9]

Holsinger thought George Horton was one of the bravest men he ever knew. Just three days earlier, Horton was shot through the arm during the battle of South Mountain. He refused to be treated at a field hospital and simply tied a handkerchief around the wound. When pressed about why he didn't go to a hospital, Horton stated, "When I go to the hospital, I will have something to take me there."

Thirty-six years later, Frank Holsinger wrote the following, "The names of Horton and Waltz are unknown to history. They are two of the grand immortals that were not born to die. They may not emblazon a page of history, but their heroism is impressed on the tablets of the memories of their companions. When the warfare of the world is over, when time strikes records with eternity, their deathless spirits will rise, beautiful from their urns of death and chambers of decay, to join the grand immortality." [10]

Holsinger made his way to the corner of the Cornfield fence and took a defensive position by a large black oak tree in the East Woods, where he fired volleys into the Cornfield and the meadow beyond. Some of the other Hopewell Rifles soldiers who were not cut down near the Cornfield fence were firing volleys from behind trees near a rock ledge 50 yards behind Hollinger. Frank's position afforded an opportunity to see much of the battlefield. He later wrote, "looking down the Pike (Dunker Church Road) I could see the Rebels coming up on the double quick in rear of the Batteries in front of the Dunker Church and passing into the meadow in front of the Church. I believe at times as the smoke lifted, 5000 rebels were under my vision and within reach of our fire." Holsinger recalled seeing James Cleaver and George Juda pushing their way through the woods on his far left, exchanging volleys with Confederates who had taken defensive positions among the trees in the East Woods. During one exchange, a Confederate skirmisher fired at them from behind a stump. Juda leaped forward toward the Rebel and "shot him dead before he could reload." [11]

George V.A. Juda was born around 1841. He mustered in the Hopewell Rifles company of the 8th PA Reserves in June 1861. George was taken prisoner during the withdrawal from Mechanicsville in June 1862 and later exchanged. He suffered a severe wound in May 1864, during the battle of Spotsylvania, a few days before the end of his enlistment, George died at a hospital in Washington, DC, on June 25th, 1864. Little else is known about George other than being listed as a Bedford County resident in the Pennsylvania Civil War Archives and in other records. He is buried at the Arlington National Cemetery. [12]

James Cleaver is pictured after the Civil War. His father, Charles Cleaver, was the minister at the Barndollar Methodist Church in Bloody Run (Everett) from 1860 to 1862. James mustered as a 1st Sgt. in the Hopewell Rifles in June 1861. James suffered a leg wound at the battle of Fredericksburg in December 1862. He was promoted to 2nd Lt. in October 1863. James was wounded a 2nd time in May 1864 at the battle of Spotsylvania. His obituary stated he was wounded 4 times. Available records list only two wounds. This is a good example of wounds not always being recorded during the Civil War. [13]

Nearby General Joseph Hooker, commanding general of the 1st Corps, was being treated for a wound. Corporal John Q. Leighty, a 23-year-old blacksmith from Hopewell, and three other men rushed the general to the rear. Fighting Joe Hooker was a major figure in the Civil War and was promoted by Lincoln to commanding general of the Union Army in early 1863. Tragically, both of John Q. Leighty's feet were blown off by a shell from a rebel battery while returning to his unit, after carrying Hooker from the field. Leighty is buried in the Antietam National Cemetery. [14]

Brigade commander Col. Albert Magilton wrote in his official report after the battle, "I have to speak particularly of the gallant conduct of Major Baily and his regiment (8th PA Reserves). It was this regiment that stood its grounds manfully and served as the rally point for the rest of the brigade that at one time had broken." [15]

An 1865 book written on the PA Reserves stated, "The Cornfield and its ghastly harvest which the reaper had gathered in those fatal hours remained finally with us. The dead are strewn so thickly that as you ride over it, you cannot guide your horse's steps too carefully. Pale and bloody faces are everywhere upturned. They are sad and terrible, but there is nothing which makes one's heart beat so quickly as the imploring look of sorely wounded men who beckon wearily for help, which you cannot stay to give." [16]

From 6 am to 9 am, the 30-acre cornfield changed hands no less than 6 times. One vicious charge was answered by an equally vicious counter-charge.

Continue East on Mansfield Avenue for 0.4 miles toward the Cornfield sector of the battlefield.

Around 0.2 miles from the 8th PA Reserves Monument, you will enter the northern edge of the East Woods. The Hopewell Rifles fought in the wooded area to the right just before Mansfield Avenue veers left toward Smoketown Road.

Right on Smoketown Road & proceed 0.2 miles through the East Woods.

Right on Cornfield Avenue & proceed 0.3 miles and pull into the Cornfield parking lot on the right.

The Cornfield Trail marker is 200 feet to the right of the parking lot. For a good perspective of the battlefield, walk on the trail to where the 8th PA Reserves were positioned. Once you reach the north edge of the Cornfield, go right toward the East Woods.

View from the north edge of the Cornfield, looking toward the East Woods. Walking down the left side of the rail fencing through an opening not shown in this photograph is the best choice. The 11th & 107th PA Regiments also entered the Cornfield along this path.

View of where the 8th PA Reserves were located near the edge of the Cornfield.

Return to the Cornfield trail entrance marker by the parking lot to tour where Bedford County soldiers in the 107th and 11th PA Infantry regiments emerged from the southern edge of Cornfield.

Once you reach the Cornfield trail entrance, a good option is to walk along Cornfield Avenue to view the brigade markers for the 107th & 11th PA Regiments then continue toward the southeastern corner of the Cornfield and loop back to the parking lot along the rail fence on the edge of Cornfield.

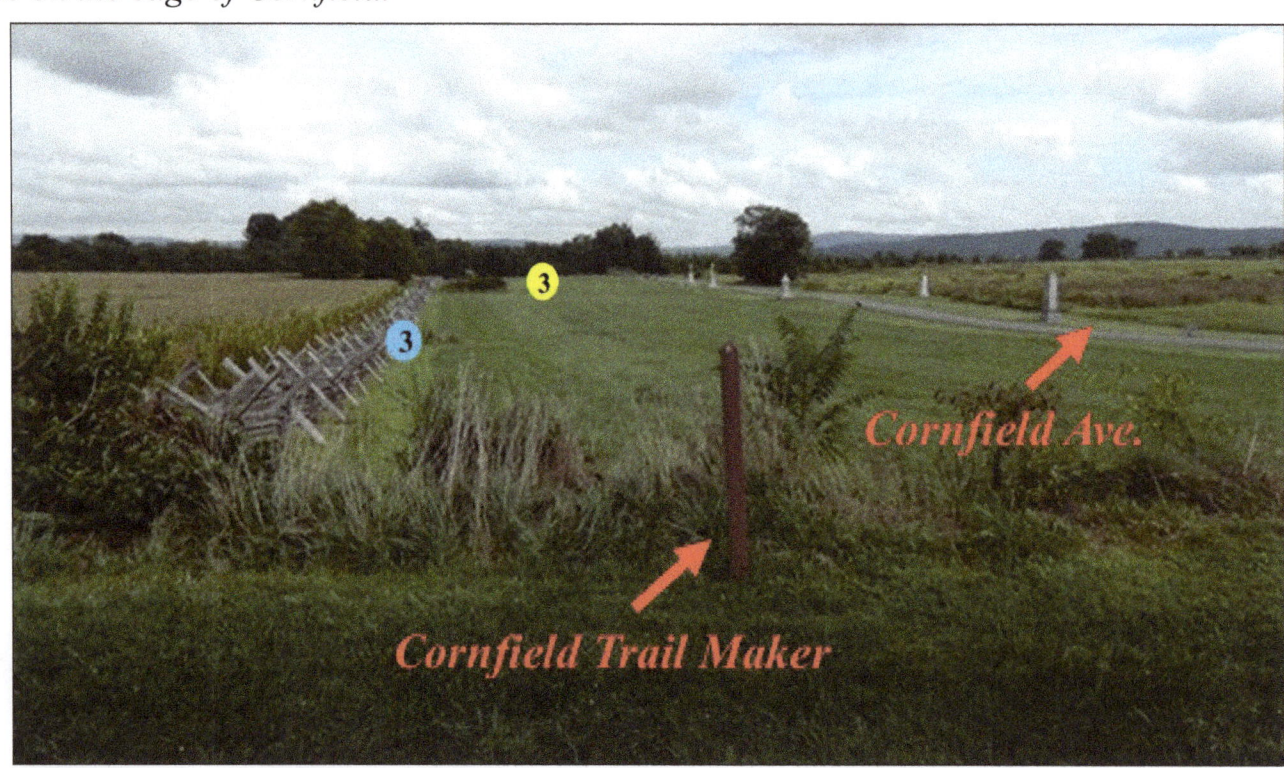

The 107th PA Infantry was one of the first six Union regiments to emerge from the southern edge of the Cornfield very early in the morning. Captain MacThompson of the 107th PA wrote the following in his official army report, "At early dawn, we moved forward through a narrow strip of timber (North Woods) gained the night previous, into a plowed field, on the opposite side of where Thompson's Battery had just taken position. Advancing halfway across the field to within easy supporting distance of the battery, we halted for about five minutes, the enemy's shell and round shot flying about us like hail, killing and wounding some of our poor fellows, but not injuring the morale of the regiment in the least. Shortly we were again advancing, and passing the batteries, over a clover field, and reached the spot so frequently mentioned in the reports of this battle - the Cornfield. Deploying in line, we entered the Cornfield and pushed rapidly through to the farther side. Here we found, in different positions, three full brigades of the enemy. We opened fire immediately upon those in front, and in fifteen minutes compelled them to fall back. After receiving reinforcements, the Rebels soon regained their position, and an unequal conflict of nearly three-quarters of an hour resulted in forcing us back through the Cornfield. Our brigade had, however, done its work. We had held at bay a force of the enemy numerically five times our superior for considerably more than an hour, and at one time driving them. We were then relieved by reinforcements coming up and retired to the rear. During the remainder of the battle, we were held in reserve and were not again called into action except to support batteries." [17]

In the Cornfield, the 107th was positioned directly next to one of the most famous and highly regarded Union Army units of the Civil War, the Iron Brigade. Major Rufus Dawes, commander of one of the Iron Brigade regiments, the 6th Wisconsin Regiment, described the following of their advance in the Cornfield, "We climbed the fence, moved across the open space and pushed on into the cornfield. I halted the left wing and ordered them to lie down on the ground. The bullets began to clip through the corn, and spin through the soft furrows–thick, almost as hail. Shells burst around us, the fragments tearing up the ground, and canister whistled through the corn above us. At the front edge of the cornfield was a low Virginia rail fence. Before the corn were open fields, beyond which was a strip of woods surrounding a little church, the Dunkard church. As we appeared at the edge of the corn, a long line of men in butternut and gray rose up from the ground. Simultaneously, the hostile battle lines opened a tremendous fire upon each other. I cannot say men fell; they were knocked out of the ranks by the dozens." [18]

Lt. James Thomas of the 107th PA wrote a letter to his father the day after the battle. He stated 18 soldiers in the 107th PA Infantry were killed and 65 wounded, including 2nd Lt. George W. Z. Black who had suffered wounds through both legs that surgeons hoped could be saved from amputation. Lt. Black volunteered in the 107th PA Infantry at Ray's Hill (Breezewood) six months earlier. Thomas wrote, "on some portions of the field, soldiers were lying so close you could step from body to body." Five of the eight men who held the 107th colors (battle flags) were casualties that morning, including two who lost their lives. Of the 196 soldiers in the 107th who rushed toward the Cornfield, only 113 soldiers remained who could carry a rifle two hours later.[19]

(left) Frederick L Frazey was born near Mattie. He left his home in East Providence Township when he was 21 years old to enlist in the 11th PA Infantry in September 1861. Frederick was wounded at Antietam. He recovered and returned home in March 1863 to teach school. Frederick married the following year and moved west. Frederick was a farmer and carpenter in Kansas and Illinois. He lived to be 84 and is buried in Urbana, IL.[20]

(Right) Major Rufus Dawes of the 6th Wisconsin Regiment of the Iron Brigade.

West facing view of where the 11th and 107th PA emerged from the south edge of the Cornfield.

Union soldiers gathered at a clump of trees and a rock outcropping near unburied Confederates the day after the battle. This location was 50 yards directly in front of the battle line marker of the 11th PA Infantry on a knoll near the southern edge of the Cornfield. The tree line in the distance is the West Woods.

1. At first light in the North Woods, the fields and wooded areas in front of the 11th PA Infantry erupted violently. Shortly before 6:30, Bedford County soldiers in this regiment advanced toward the killing grounds of the Cornfield. William Henry Locke volunteered in the 11th PA Infantry in November 1861. In an 1868 memoir, he described what he witnessed on the morning of September 17th, "Up from among the stalks of corn, sprung ranks of armed men; while from sheltered woods and every rising knoll, the artillery of friend and foe was sending forth shot and shell." The first Union regiments to emerge from the southern edge of the Cornfield were viciously cut down by rifle fire from Georgia regiments lined up less than a couple hundred yards away. Shortly after, Brigadier General James Ricketts received an order to send in his best brigade to replace the broken and depleted regiments of the initial assault.[21] The 11th PA Infantry was part of Hartsuff's Brigade that was ordered forward.

2. Hartsuff's Brigade rushed on the double quick over open ground under heavy fire. As they pressed through the Cornfield, fragments of Union brigades shattered by rebel fire streamed past them to the rear. Hartsuff's Brigade collided with Confederate regiments from Georgia and Louisiana and drove the Rebels out of the Cornfield back to their original battle line.[22]

3. William Henry Locke described the 11th PA Infantry advance to the crest of a small hill a short distance from the Cornfield, "No one bent before the storm. Firing first in volleys, they fired then at will, with wonderful rapidity and effect. The whole line crowned the hill and stood out darkly against the sky; but lighted and shrouded ever in flame and smoke. There, for half an hour, they held the ridge, unyielding in purpose, exhaustless in courage. There were gaps in the line, but it was nowhere bent. Their supports did not come, and they determined to win without them. They were there to win that field, and they won it. The rebel line for the second time fled through the corn and into the woods. I cannot tell how few of Hartsuff's Brigade were left when the work was done, but it was done." [23]

The marker on the left is the battle line of the 11th PA Infantry near the southern edge of the Cornfield. The same rock outcropping on the photograph on the previous page remains on the battlefield today by the clump of trees in the middle of the above photo.

At around 7:15 am, the entire Union line, including Hartsuff's Brigade, was driven back from the southern edge of the Cornfield. A fresh wave of reinforcements under Confederate General John Bell Hood stormed into the Cornfield as the Pennsylvania Reserve regiments, including Bedford County soldiers in the Hopewell Rifles company, rushed forward across the open fields of the Miller Farm to meet Hood's Rebel soldiers.

Locke recalled the following while walking through the Cornfield after the battle, "Death came to many with musket raised to the shoulder, in the very act of firing; and in falling forward, the dead soldier kept fast hold of his gun. Others, again, lay on the ground, with arms wide extended, and the last look of anguish fixed in the rigid features. In a single row, with scarcely two feet between them, were eighty-one of the enemy's dead. It was a battle-line moving forward, each man meeting death at the same instant. Such a volley, telling so fearfully on the front rank, was a complete check at that point; for there were no indications here of advance and retreat, as were seen on other parts of that ground, in the bodies of friend and foe falling together. We had only to pass up through Miller's cornfield, and into the woods beyond, to find most of the slain belonging to the Eleventh. Writing the name of each man on a slip of paper, with the number of the regiment and the letter of his company, and fastening it to coat or shirt, the graves of our comrades were so plainly marked, that when friends came to remove sons and brothers, we could point with certainty to all that remained of brave and loving hearts." [24]

Of the 1220 men and boys in Hartsuff's Brigade who advanced toward the Cornfield, 579 had become battlefield casualties, including 82 who lost their lives in a little over an hour.[25]

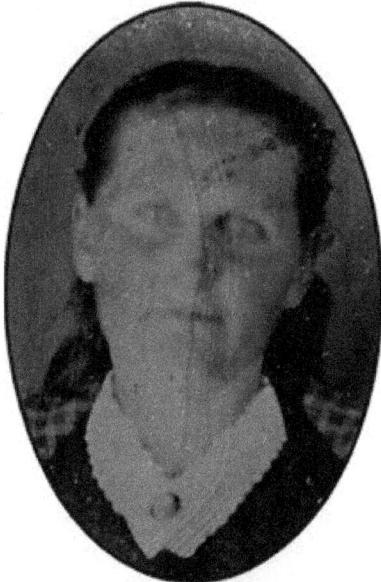

(left) Frances W. Pee left his East Providence Township home to volunteer in the 11th PA Infantry in September 1861. His wife Sarah gave birth to their first child in March 1862. Five months later, Frances was hit in the shoulder by a minie ball at Antietam. On July 1st, 1863, Francis suffered a wound above the elbow at Gettysburg and was taken prisoner. He was exchanged for a Confederate days later. Francis recovered and returned home in January 1864. Francis and Sarah were the parents of 9 children. Sarah passed in 1907 at age 62. Francis passed four years later at age 71 and was buried beside his wife in the Mt. Pleasant Cemetery near Mattie.[26]

(right) A dead Confederate soldier on the left is lying next to a recently dug grave of a Union soldier. Note the two cannon balls lodged in the large tree. The location of the photograph is approximately 100 yards north of the Smoketown Road / Mumma Farm Lane intersection. The West Woods is visible in the background.

Dunker Church sector battlefield map

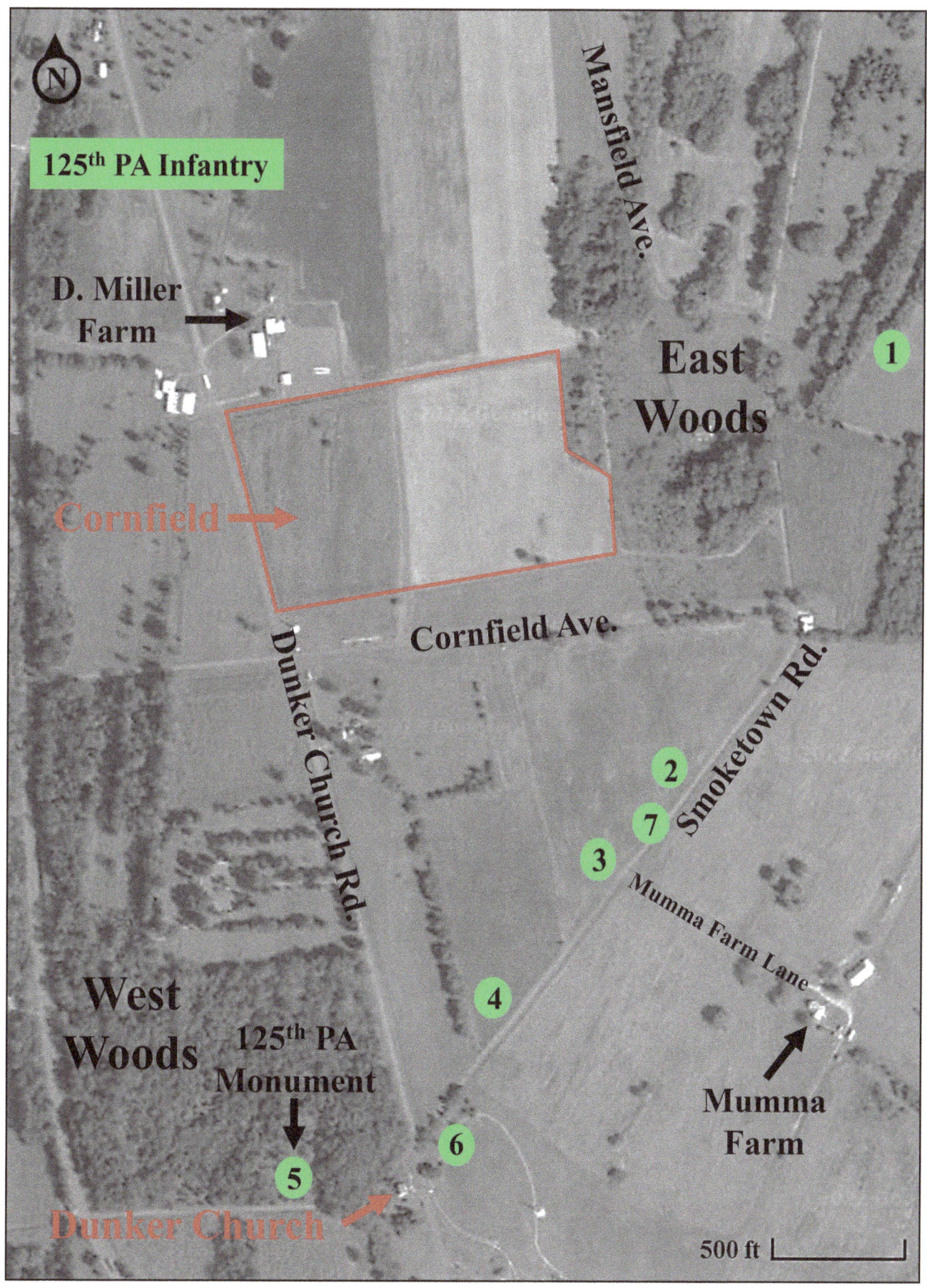

Farmers, merchants, coal miners and day laborers were among the ranks of volunteers in the 125th PA Infantry. Most were from Blair, Cambria and Huntingdon Counties. Close to 50 recruits from Bedford County were also among those who mustered in the middle of August 1862. Very few had any prior military experience.[27]

The recruits traveled by train to Harrisburg for a brief physical and a new uniform before boarding another train to Washington, DC. The next 3 weeks were filled with drill and fatigue duty. During this time, the mood in Washington grew progressively gloomy after the Union Army was routed at the 2nd Battle of Bull Run. On September 7th, the 125th PA broke camp and marched toward Frederick, MD.[28] The afternoon before the battle, 125th PA crossed Antietam creek and bivouacked near the George Lines farmhouse. That night, soldiers slept little while laying between rows of corn, preoccupied by thoughts of home and loved ones. Occasional sounds of horses neighing, dogs barking and roosters crowing co-mingled with scattered rifle fire from pickets on the front lines.[29]

Around 6:00 in the morning, the 125th began their march toward cannon and rifle fire. They halted several times before nearing the front an hour later. As they approached the East Woods, Lt. Thomas McCamant of Hollidaysburg recalled, "wounded men from the PA Reserve Regiments were being rushed past them for medical treatment in the rear. Soon, Confederate artillery shells were exploding nearby, and the Mumma Farm buildings could be seen burning in the distance.[30] Upon entering the East Woods, the 125th deployed a battle line and began witnessing the ghastly sight of men dropping rapidly in front of them.[31]

At around 8:00 am, the 125th PA approached the wooded area near the Cornfield where the dead, dying, and wounded of both armies were lying together among cornstalks cut down by rifle and cannister fire. Miles C. Huyette, a resident of Blair County in the 125th PA, later wrote on their advance through the

A dead horse lies near the southern edge of East Woods. The tree line of the East Woods stretched to Smoketown Road during the time of the battle. The rider of the horse, believed to be a Confederate Colonel, was also killed. The 125th PA Infantry crossed the ground behind the horse during their advance toward the Dunker Church.

East Woods, "A cloud of smoke hung low to the ground, and we could only see a short distance. Filling the air were the sounds, "Zipp," "Ping" and a sickening "Thud" when minie balls hit flesh and bone. The Union Army lines in front of us practically melted away, but "Johnnie Reb" was on the spot, firing at us from behind trees and ledges of rocks, keeping up a hot fire while being pressed. As clouds of smoke would lift, we could see men running, stopping to load, and firing again. We broke through the rebel line and advanced with both flanks in the air before being ordered to "Halt!" and "Lie down!" in a clover field, just to the right of the Smoketown Road." [32] The 125th was taking fire from a Confederate battery located on a limestone ledge near the Dunker Church.[33]

Take a Left out of the Cornfield parking lot & proceed 0.3 miles back to Smoketown Road.

Right on Smoketown Road & proceed 0.2 miles to Mumma Farm Lane and pull over on the right side of the road.

(right) Col. Jacob C. Higgins was born in Williamsburg in the northern end of Morrisons Cove in 1826. Though not a resident of Bedford County, Jacob was a very prominent local figure during the Civil War. He was commissioned as a colonel in the 125th PA Infantry on August 16th, 1862, a month prior to the battle of Antietam. He mustered out of the 125th at the end of the regiment enlistment period in May 1863. A little more than a month later, Jacob organized a local emergency militia that dug defensive entrenchments at the Loysburg Gap during the battle of Gettysburg, which are visible today. His name is prominently listed on the roadside marker at the site. Jacob was commissioned as a colonel in the 22nd PA Cavalry in March 1864 and led over 100 Bedford County soldiers on the largest Union army calvary charge of the war at the battle of Opequon in September 1864. Jacob provided many details of the remarkable story of the 125th Pennsylvania Infantry at Antietam.[34]

Around 8:30 am, a short advance was made to the rise by the Mumma Farm Lane, before the command was again shouted to "Halt!" and "Lie Down." Withering enemy fire forced the soldiers in the 125th to shield their faces from the splinters flying off rail fencing where they were taking cover. Nearby, the Mumma Farm buildings were burning, greatly reducing visibility.[35]

Jacob Higgins was kneeling by a fence post when the commanding general of the 1st Corps, Joseph Hooker, rode up to him at a full gallop. Hooker shouted, "what regiment is this - what is in front of you?" Higgins answered, "125th PA - Nothing but Rebels"; General Hooker pointed to West Woods and gave the command, "Advance and hold those woods." An instant later Hooker's horse was frantic with pain after being struck by several minie balls. As Higgins shouted, "General, you better get out of this," a round hit Hooker's foot. The general immediately wheeled around and galloped to the rear.[36]

Thankfully, Union artillery fire had just forced the withdrawal of the Rebel batteries near the Dunker Church. Jacob Higgins shouted "Attention" and "Forward." The men in the 125th rose and began a perilous advance across open ground, yelling the entire way down the hill as rebel soldiers from South Carolina and Georgia retreated into the West Woods.[37] Opposing Confederate General J. B. Gordon described this advance of the 125th, "it was evidently a new regiment, unscathed by battle. Its members were novices in the sufferings of war, perhaps never in their lives under fire. Their clothing and

This photograph of Confederate dead near the Dunker Church is one of the most iconic images of the Civil War. The day before, Bedford County soldiers in the 125th PA Regiment passed through the missing rail fence section on the right-side of this photograph and advanced another 500 feet in the West Woods.

This image shows the same abandoned limber chest and dead Confederate soldiers lying nearby as in the top photograph.

accouterments were new, as if worn only on parade. Their bayonets were as bright as household silver. Bravely advancing, they kept step, bearing aloft their colors, new from ladies' hands; the band played gloriously, and every officer was in his place." [38]

6. Jacob Higgins recalled, "The enemy in our immediate front fell back very stubbornly. We crossed the pike (Dunker Church Road) and halted to straighten our line.[38] We advanced a short distance in the woods and halted again to examine the enemy's position. I found him in force in my front and on my right. On looking around I discovered myself without support either in my rear or right, and, being the only mounted officer present, I gave my horse to Lieutenant Higgins (his brother), and instructed him to ride back to the general, inform him of my situation, and ask him to send support immediately, or I would be unable to hold my position, and that the enemy would certainly flank me and cut me off, my command being at this time in advance of the whole corps. I ordered Captain McKeage to lead the advance cautiously to the crest of a small hill. The regiment soon became engaged with the enemy,

Proceed 0.2 miles on Smoketown Road to Dunker Church Road.

Left on Dunker Church Road and immediately park on the right side of the road in front of the Dunker Church.

On the north-side of the Dunker Church (to the right when facing the Dunker Church from the road) is a dirt path. This path will lead to the 125th Pennsylvania Regiment Monument. The monument is approximately 500 feet in back of the Church. The battle line of the 125th PA was roughly positioned along this path during multiple Confederate assaults in the West Woods.

3.

This photograph of Knap's Battery was taken around 100 yards in front of the Dunker Church, facing slightly more toward the northeast than the bottom photo on the previous page. The Cornfield and the East Woods are in the distant background. If the photographs on the previous page and the above photograph were laid next to each other, a near panoramic image would be provided of the advance of the 125th PA from the Mumma Farm Lane to the West Woods the previous day.

who were advancing on my front in force, and I gave the command to commence firing. A most destructive fire caused the enemy to halt. I held him here for some time, until I discovered two regiments of them moving around my right, while a brigade charged on my front." [39]

Miles Huyette provided a description of the 125th PA advance into the West Woods, "Dead and wounded lay about in every conceivable position; the trees freshly scarred and broken branches hanging and littering the ground. The walls of the church were scarred by bullets and daylight shone through holes made by shells. We could look to the left and see rebel formations being made to drive us out, and our regiment was alone in the rebel lines without support. A partial crossfire combed the ground and made the fallen dead leaves move as if alive and active, and the slaughter began. When we opened fire, the crash, cheers, and cries of the wounded made a fearful din, and it was impossible to hear orders. No words can convey to the inexperienced a comprehensive idea of the surging and plunging of two great armies in deadly battle, a hurricane of death sweeping the earth. The cross fires caused the line to disintegrate, first from the right and extended to the left; the first I knew was to be almost alone and a mass of yelling and firing rebels only about fifty yards distant." [40] Four separate Rebel assaults in the West Woods were successfully resisted with heavy losses before the 125th PA was forced to withdrawal.[41]

Higgins described the retreat from the West Woods, "The firing was terrific on both sides. Our color-bearer fell with a ball through his brain, and one by one all the color-guard went down. I ordered the Adjutant down the line to direct the men to fall back, or they would be all captured. By this time that rebel yell, so well-known to us afterward, sounded above the din of battle. On they came in solid columns like an avalanche that threatened to sweep all before it, yet the regiment would not move. I yelled at the top of my voice, but the men kept firing away into the surging mass in their front until the Confederate column came so close as to shout for us to surrender. The 125th then broke on a run to the rear." [42] In his official report, Higgins stated, "On looking around and finding no support in sight, I was compelled to retire. Had I remained in my position two minutes longer, I would have lost my whole command." [43]

Higgins recalled the following incredible incident as the retreat neared the Dunker Church, "A Confederate regiment was marching in a column of fours past the rear of the church and our regiment was running toward a Union Artillery battery (in front of the Dunker Church). We intersected the Confederate regiment right at its colors. I raised my hand to seize the flag, but something told me I had better not, and I dropped my hand and jostled through the ranks. Not a word was spoken. I asked the opposing Confederate General John D. Imboden, after the war, how that could possibly happen, and he stated they thought we were Confederates charging that battery and (early in the war) many of their men wore blue coats, and since the rest of their column was right on our heels, they took for granted we were Confederates. If I had taken their colors, more than likely we would all have been captured. We went through unmolested, and I called to our men to run between the sections of the cannons (across the Dunker Church Road). Just as we were passing, I saw the gunners ram two charges of canister into each gun and fire into the gray column. They cut swaths through the (rebel) ranks, but it did not appear to check them in the least. On they came, and the battery had to limber up (cannons were hitched to artillery horses), and we all went back at a lively gait about two-thirds of the way across the field" [44]

The 125th was reforming when a Union artillery officer galloped up to Higgins and pleaded in an excited tone, "Colonel, for God's sake, come and save my battery. The enemy is charging on it, and I have no support. My horses are all shot down, I cannot get my guns away and pointed toward his battery." Higgins shouted, "attention column forward - double-quick - march!" In very short time, soldiers in the 125th approached the battery under a storm of bullets, just as the rebels had reached the cannons. Higgins wrote, "We poured a terrible fire into them with telling effect, and the few Union artillerymen that were left with the battery redoubled their energy. If they ever did any fast firing, it was then. We soon drove the enemy back with great slaughter." [45] The 125th defended this position for the rest of the day. By late morning, the battle shifted to the Sunken Road and later in the afternoon to the Burnside Bridge sectors of the battlefield.

Levi Decker, a native of Hopewell Township, recalled his story of the withdrawal from the West Woods in the 125th PA Regimental history book, "at the bluff of rocks (in the West Woods) near Dunker church, while firing, I got my first wound, a bullet through my left shoulder, and on our way back, at the Pike (Dunker Church Road) I got my second wound, a bullet through my left arm. I was still able to travel and got about half-way from the Pike (Dunker Church Road) to the battery (the rescued battery referenced in the previous paragraph) when I got my third wound from the left flank of the enemy, a bullet in my right hip, which fetched me to the ground. I laid there between the lines probably two or three hours, until I recovered from the shock, and then got up and made my way painfully through the line of battle at the Cornfield and down through the woods to the big spring, where I got my wounds dressed. When the Confederates shelled it, I crossed the field over to the road at the woods and got into an ambulance, which took me to a house in the rear, out of range of the Confederate fire, where I laid until September 27th, and was taken to Frederick City Hospital, where I remained until discharged, December 17th, 1862, unfit for further duty, and this ended my military service." [46]

No roll call was taken the morning of the battle. Colonel Higgins believed less than 700 of his men carried a rifle at Antietam on September 17th.[47] A month and a day after they were organized, 226 men and boys in the 125th PA had been killed, wounded, or were missing. Most of the casualties took place during the 20 minutes of horrific fighting in the West Woods.[48]

(left) Miles Huyette on the left pictured with his grandson circa WW1.[49]

(right) Photo of the 125th PA Monument. The Dunker Church is visible in the background on the right.[50]

(left) 125th Pennsylvania veterans at the dedication of the regiment's Antietam monument on September 17th, 1904. The monument features a likeness of Sgt. George A. Simpson, who was killed in the West Woods. The flag shown in this photograph was the actual flag that Sergeant Simpson saved from capture during the battle.

*(left) William Kean Campbell in his uniform during the war. William and his wife Anna are also pictured later in life. They married in 1856 and Anna gave birth to her third child 3 weeks before her husband fought at Antietam. William later wrote a letter to his daughter of his experiences in the 125th PA Infantry. He stated, "Our regiment advanced further into the woods than any other regiment. On the march (to Antietam) I took (came down with) typhoid fever and was ordered into the ambulance but refused - remained (with the 125th PA) until after the battle and was sent to the Hagerstown Hospital - from there to Camp Curtain, at Harrisburg – where I remained until December 21st, 1862 – when I was honorably discharged – got home on Christmas Day. **I did what I could.**" William and Anna were the parents of 7 more children born after the war. William passed at age 70 in 1898 and was buried at the Bedford Cemetery. Anna lived to be 83 and was buried beside her husband in 1922.*[51]

(right) David Harclerode is pictured outside his house in Earlston, near Everett and in the photo on the bottom right. David suffered a wound while climbing over a fence on the 125th PA advance toward the Dunker Church. A bullet entered his right hip and passed through the groin. There were so many casualties during the battle, some soldiers waited days while surgeons attended to the most seriously wounded. David laid on the battlefield, where he was in and out of consciousness for 4 days and 4 nights before being attended to. Whenever he came out of consciousness, David would look at the pocket watch of the dead Confederate soldier next to him to keep track of time. David later told his family that he did not take the pocket watch, because he feared he would be thought of as a thief if it was found on his dead body. He recovered in a hospital in Washington, D.C. before rejoining the 125th. David mustered out in May 1863 and returned to Everett where he spent the rest of his life farming. He suffered from vision problems he believed were partially the result of lying outdoors on the Antietam Battlefield. He passed in 1911 at age 69 and is buried in the Everett Cemetery.[52]

(right) Michael B. Breneman grew up in Huntington County. He was 24 years old when he volunteered with his brother George in the 125th Pennsylvania Infantry in August 1862. Both brothers were wounded during the battle of Antietam. Michael was hit by a Minie ball in the left leg and carried out of the West Woods by two fellow soldiers. He was taken to the nearby Poffenberger barn, where he remained for ten days. Michael returned home and taught school the following winter on crutches. His brother was not as fortunate. George succumbed to his wounds on November 10th, 1862. Michael graduated from Jefferson Medical College in Philadelphia in 1870 and became a well-known doctor in Saxton. He married Anna Shaffer in 1869 and they were the parents of 5 children who survived into adulthood. Michael lived to be 82 years old and was buried in the Fockler Cemetery in Saxton in 1921.[53]

Benjamin and Caroline Jamison are pictured with their grandchildren. Benjamin was 19 when he left Snake Spring Valley to volunteer in the 125th PA Infantry in August 1862. He suffered a thigh wound at the battle of Antietam. While recovering in Harrisburg, he contracted Typhoid Fever and became so delirious he did not recognize his father, who stayed at his bedside for 8 weeks. In January, his father received permission to take him home to recover. Benjamin was too weak to walk and did not regain saneness until April 1863. The regimental enlistment period ended the following month. After recovering, Benjamin volunteered in the 110th PA Regiment in February 1864. Four months later, he was captured during the Battle of Cold Harbor and spent the next nine months in hellish POW camps in Andersonville, GA and Florence, SC. After being released, he was hospitalized for a month before returning home. Benjamin married Caroline Whetstone in 1867 and they raised a large family of 10 children. Benjamin was a schoolteacher and a Justice of the Peace in Loysburg. Caroline passed in 1907. Benjamin died at age 77 and was buried beside his wife in St. John's Reformed Cemetery in Loysburg in 1920.[54]

David R Shorthill was a 31-year-old miner who lived in Broad Top City when he volunteered in the 125th PA regiment a month before Antietam. He left behind his wife, Margaret Richards Shorthill, and 5 small children. David was shot in the abdomen, just above the hip in the field between the Dunker Church and the Mumma Farm Lane. Family tradition stated he was left for dead on the battlefield but later regained consciousness and crawled to a fence row where he was found. David was taken to Hoffman's barn a couple miles from the battlefield where hundreds of other wounded soldiers were being treated. A few days later, a farmer gave David and another wounded soldier a ride in a hay wagon to Hagerstown for medical care. During his lengthy recovery, his wife and children stayed with Margaret's parents in Coalmont. David returned home in March 1863. A couple months later, David was asked by his former captain, William Wallace, to recruit a group of men for an emergency militia to defend the gap on Sideling Hill at Waterfall during the Gettysburg Campaign. After the Rebel army retreated from PA, Shorthill returned to the mines in the Broad Top before leaving for the gold fields in Montana in 1864. David was part of a group that discovered gold on the Yellowstone River. David and Margaret were the parents of three more children born after the war and lived prosperous lives near present day Yellowstone National Park. Margaret passed at age 64 in 1898. David passed in 1906 at age 75 and was buried beside his wife in Park County, Montana.[55]

Photographs of the Hoffman Barn. The barn was a temporary field hospital for hundreds of wounded soldiers. Virtually every barn and church within several miles of Sharpsburg became a makeshift medical facility to care for the over 20,000 battlefield casualties suffered during the battle.[56]

The story of another soldier in the 125th PA who grew up in the Broad Top did not end as well as it did for the Shorthill family. Below is an article published in the Altoona Tribune on October 2nd, 1862, on the death of James A Kelly during the withdrawal from the West Woods. His wife Jane gave birth to their first son, John A. Kelly, the month after her husband was killed.[57]

LOCAL ITEMS.

FUNERAL OF CORPORAL JOHN A. KELLY.— On Saturday evening last, Mr. Joshua Kelly, of this place, returned from the battle-field of Antietam, with the remains of his son, Corporal John A. Kelly, of Company D. 125th Reg't P. V., who fell, mortally wounded, in the early part of the engagement. It is said by his companions that he was bayoneted, before he died, by a rebel who came up with him on the field. The day after the battle his body was found by Wm. A. B. Laub, of the same company, who had been detailed to help bury the dead, who interred the remains as decently as possible and marked the grave.

The funeral took place at three o'clock on Sunday afternoon, and was attended by four companies of the militia, the Good Will Fire Company, and a very large concourse of citizens. His remains were deposited in the circle in the centre of Fair View Cemetery, which, as our readers will remember, has been tendered by the Association as the burial ground of all soldiers from Altoona and vicinity who may die or be killed during the war.

Another local story exists of parents traveling to Maryland to bring back the body of a son. William Malone was 24 years old when he volunteered in the Hopewell Rifles Company of the 8th PA Reserves in June 1861. His enlistment paperwork stated he was 5'7" tall with blue eyes, dark hair, light complexion and was working as a miner. He was wounded near the Cornfield at Antietam and died 5 weeks later on October 24th, 1862. His stepfather George Bowers and mother Eliza Atkinson Malone Bowers drove a wagon to where he was buried, exhumed his body, and brought William back to Bedford County for burial in Saint Paul's Cemetery in Yellow Creek. His brother Charles Malone was taken prisoner during the battle of Globe Tavern in Virginia in August 1864 and died 4 months later at the Salisbury POW camp in North Carolina. There is no record of where Charles was buried. A third son, John Malone, was also captured and taken to Andersonville, but survived the war.[58]

*(left) Pastor David Long
1820-1881*

*(Right) Frank Holsinger
1836-1916*

After the battle, Frank Holsinger of the 8th PA Reserves recalled counting 100 balls in one fence rail at the Cornfield. Frank's best friend in the Hopewell Rifles, James Gates, was in grave condition from wounds suffered at the edge of the Cornfield. While being treated in a nearby field hospital, James became close to the pastor of the Dunker Church, David Long. James Gates succumbed to his wounds on October 16th, 1862 and was taken back to Bedford County for burial in St. Paul's Cemetery in Yellow Creek. Frank Holsinger went to the home of Pastor Long to provide the news of James' passing. While Frank was there, he met his future wife, the daughter of the Dunker Church pastor. Frank Holsinger and Mary Long were married on November 20th, 1867, and moved to Kansas City soon after. They returned to Sharpsburg many times during their lives to visit family.[59]

Damage from rifle fire and cannon shells are visible in the Dunker Church in this photograph taken shortly after the battle.

Harpers Ferry - September 13th - 15th 1862

The Union garrison defending Harpers Ferry surprised Robert E. Lee twice during the first attempted Confederate invasion of Pennsylvania. Lee expected the isolated garrison at Harpers Ferry would evacuate once they realized they were cut off from the rest of the Union Army. They did not. While in Frederick, MD, Stonewall Jackson was dispatched to surround the garrison and force a quick surrender and reunite with Lee's main Confederate army group. Jackson's forces arrived at Harpers Ferry on September 12th and expected the Union garrison to surrender. They refused. Two days later, Confederates forces were driven off the passes at South Mountain, putting Lee's divided army in peril. On September 15th, Stonewall Jackson opened a heavy artillery bombardment from the high ground surrounding Harpers Ferry and finally forced the Union garrison to surrender. This delay nearly resulted in the destruction of the Confederate army at Antietam. The rebel forces of A.P. Hill, the last to leave Harpers Ferry, arrived just in time to reinforce beleaguered Confederate Army lines as they were about to be overrun near the Burnside Bridge.

The 3rd Maryland PHB Infantry was one of the Union regiments who defended Harpers Ferry. Over 30 Bedford County soldiers were enlisted in the regiment at the time of the battle. All soldiers who were at Harpers Ferry on September 15th would have been captured. It is highly likely many more than the 7 Bedford County soldiers listed on the next page were taken prisoner on that day, but additional POW records have not been located.

This photograph of Harpers Ferry was taken on the Maryland Heights side of the Potomac River after the bridge was destroyed by retreating Confederates in 1861. This bridge was destroyed and rebuilt several times during the war.

Harpers Ferry - known Bedford Co. casualty listing

Name	Muster Age	Rank	State	Regiment	Company	Casualty
Hendershot, Samuel C	27	Pvt.	MD	3rd PHB Infantry	C	POW
Karns, Jabez	28	Pvt.	MD	3rd PHB Infantry	C	POW
Linn, Hugh	52	Pvt.	MD	3rd PHB Infantry	B	POW
Linn, Riley	17	Pvt.	MD	3rd PHB Infantry	B	POW
Linn, William	14	Pvt.	MD	3rd PHB Infantry	B	POW
Smith, Nathan P R	18	Pvt.	MD	3rd PHB Infantry	B	POW
Sponsler, George W	18	Pvt.	MD	3rd PHB Infantry	C	POW

(left) John F. Lowery was 37 years old when he volunteered in the 3rd Maryland PHB Infantry in September 1861. He left behind a wife and a small child at his Broad Top Township home. John mustered out of the army in February 1864.[1]

(right) John Schetrompf was born in Germany in 1841 and came to America with his parents as a young boy. He volunteered in the 3rd MD PHB in October 1861. Two brothers enlisted in the 3rd MD PHB after him, George in January 1862, and Peter in October 1863. All 3 brothers survived the war.[2]

(left) Joseph B. Smith grew up in Southampton Township. He was 21 years old when he mustered in the 3rd MD PHB Infantry in February 1862. Joseph mustered out after the war ended in May 1865.[3]

(right) George W. Sponsler was 18 when he left his Everett home with his 16-year-old brother Solomon to volunteer in the 3rd MD PHB Infantry. George was captured at Harpers Ferry. No record of Solomon being captured has been located. Both mustered out at the end of the war in 1865.[4]

Harpers Ferry Map

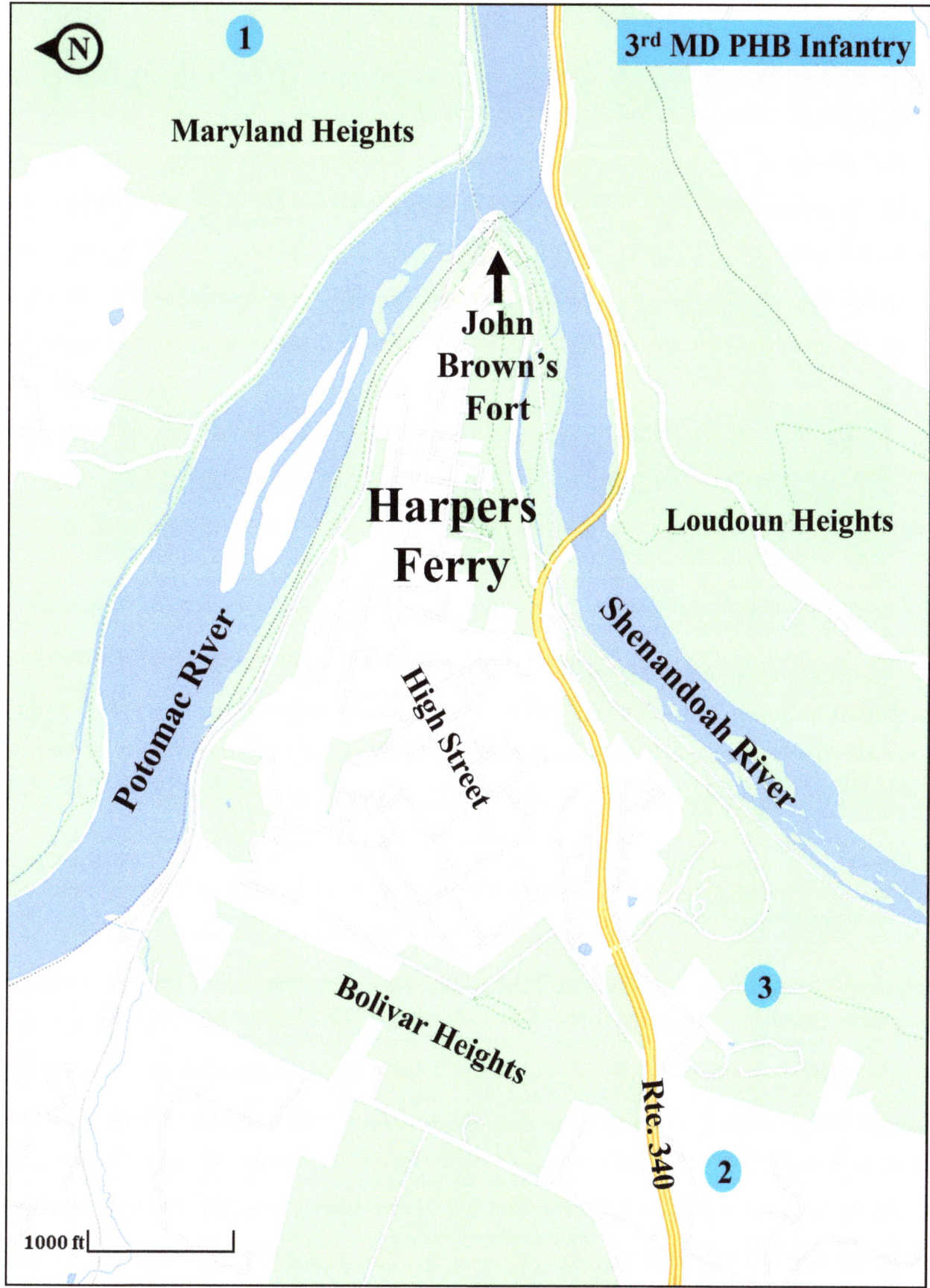

Photograph circa 1860 of the fire engine house at the Harpers Ferry Armory, more commonly referred to as John Brown's Fort. John Brown and his followers were barricaded in this building during their ill-fated raid to seize weapons and arm slaves in October 1859. John Brown's Raid inflamed pro-slavery sentiments in the South and was one of the most famous events leading up to the Civil War.

Tour begins at John Brown's Fort - 814 Shenandoah Street Harpers Ferry, WV 25425

Across the river on the left at John Brown's Fort is Maryland Heights. The top of Maryland Heights can be reached via a 4.5-mile moderate hike on the Maryland Heights Trail. Please visit the NPS.gov website if interested in directions and a trail map.

Harpers Ferry was strategically important because of the confluence of the Shenandoah and Potomac Rivers on its banks, but defending the town was problematic. Harper Ferry sat in a bowl surrounded by three heights. Maryland Heights was the tallest at 1400 feet, Loudoun Heights rose up 1100 feet and Bolivar Heights stood 300 feet above the town.[5]

① Bedford County soldiers in the 3rd MD PHB Infantry were part of the brigade that defended Maryland Heights during the battle. On the morning of September 13th, two brigades of veteran Confederate soldiers scrambled up the steep terrain of Maryland Heights. Unfortunately, Colonel Ford, the brigade commander of the 3rd MD PHB, was ill and was not able to scale the heights to direct the troops defending Maryland Heights. Ford sent Major Hewitt in his place, who had little military experience. The first rebel assault was repulsed, but confusion reigned on the Union line during a second attack around 9 am. Some Union soldiers defending the front-line breastwork were told the order to fall back had been given, and they began to stream back. Hewitt later said no such order was given and claimed he stated if compelled, the Union soldiers on the front line were to retire in good order. By the time the order was clarified, rebel soldiers had already climbed over the breastwork defenses. This miscommunication was unfortunate because at the time the mostly green Union soldiers on top of Maryland Heights were mounting a spirited defense and were holding their own against the more experienced Confederate troops.[6]

1863 painting of Harpers Ferry by William MacLeod. The soldiers in the foreground are on Maryland Heights where the 3rd MD PHB was positioned on September 13th. The next two days, they defended Bolivar Heights near the Shenandoah River.

View from a hill above Harpers Ferry after the bridge was rebuilt during the Civil War. Maryland Heights is across the river on the left and Loudoun Heights is on the right.

From John Brown's Fort proceed 50 yards to High Street.

Right on High Street & proceed for 1.8 miles.

Right onto 340 South & proceed 0.3 miles.

Left into the Clarion Inn hotel (address: 4328 William L Wilson Fwy, Harpers Ferry, WV 25425).

When visiting some Civil War sites, you realize not every battlefield is a well-marked National Park similar to Gettysburg and Antietam. There are no Civil War markers on this section of Bolivar Heights. When you take a left into the Clarion Inn hotel, proceed to the end of the parking lot and park your car. You will see tennis courts shown on the bottom photograph. The area on the left of the tennis courts is the crest of Bolivar Heights and is near one end of the battle line of 3rd Maryland PHB on September 14th. The battle line of the 3rd MD PHB was spread thin over another half mile southwest of this location. Today, beyond the tennis courts, a recreational park extends along Bolivar Heights and can be entered for a fee.

Colonel Dixon Miles, the commander of the Union garrison at Harpers Ferry, chose not to defend Loudoun Heights because he did not believe artillery pieces could be moved up its slopes which were nearly vertical in places. This was an unfortunate miscalculation. On the morning of September 14th, the Confederates cut a road to the top of Loudoun Heights and by 1:00 pm five rebel cannons opened fire on Harpers Ferry. An hour later, two hundred Confederate soldiers used heavy ropes to pull the first cannons up the steep slopes of Maryland Heights, and the town was bombarded from two directions. Meanwhile, Union soldiers were feverously erecting crude entrenchments on Bolivar Heights about a mile west of the town while Confederate artillery was raining destruction from above. Over the previous

year, over 30 Bedford County soldiers traveled to Cumberland, MD, to volunteer in the 3rd Maryland PHB Infantry. These soldiers were on the extreme left of the Union lines and were spread thin along a rugged section of Bolivar Heights that officers assumed would discourage a rebel assault. This was a second miscalculation. At 3:00 pm, five Confederate brigades under A.P. Hill advanced along the Shenandoah River. The 3rd MD PHB was attacked by three brigades in their front, while two brigades moved along the riverbank in an attempt to turn the left flank of the Union lines. Union reinforcements were shifted to support the 3rd MD PHB and the overwhelming rebel force of A.P. Hill was repulsed. Hostilities ceased as darkness blanketed Harpers Ferry and the beleaguered Union garrison managed to delay surrendering another day.[7]

That same evening, Bedford County soldiers in the 8th PA Reserves and the 107th PA Infantry were part of the Union force that drove the Confederates off Turner's Gap at South Mountain. The stubborn fighting at Harpers Ferry delayed Stonewall Jackson's forces from reuniting with Robert E. Lee's main army group. These actions resulted in the offensive initiative of the Rebel invasion of Pennsylvania being lost and set up the epic battle of Antietam three days later.

Early the next morning before dawn, the 3rd MD PHB and four other regiments were shifted to form a new battle-line perpendicular to Bolivar Heights that stretched to the Shenandoah River to defend

Exit Clarion Inn hotel.

Right onto 340 North & proceed 0.3 miles.

Right on Shoreline Drive.

Immediate right on Campground Road & proceed 0.2 miles.

Left on Murphy Road and proceed 0.1 miles to the entrance of the Murphy Farm Park.
The new battle line for the 3rd MD PHB was near the entrance in the below photograph.

the Union left from being flanked. Seventy Confederate cannons renewed the bombardment at 6 am. Union cannons responded in kind, but soon began running out of ammunition. Confederate infantry units were preparing to charge the Union line on Bolivar Heights when Col. Miles recognized the situation was hopeless and a flag of truce was raised in the Union lines.[8]

Among the 3rd Maryland PHB Infantry soldiers taken prisoner was Hugh Linn, a 54-year-old farmer from Robinsonville in Monroe Township and his two sons, 18-year-old Riley and William who had turned 15 the previous April.[9]

After terms of Surrender were completed, Stonewall Jackson and A.P. Hill rode into town. Union soldiers in Bolivar Heights were eager to get a glimpse of the famous Stonewall Jackson and lined the road as he approached. Afterward, the following description of Stonewall was provided by one of the captured soldiers, "He was dressed in the coarsest kind of homespun, seedy and dirty at that. He wore an old hat which any Northern beggar would consider an insult to have offered him. His general appearance was in no respect to be distinguished from the mongrel, bare-footed crew who follow his fortunes. I had heard much of the decayed appearance of the rebel soldiers, but such a looking crowd! Ireland, in her worst straits, could present no parallel, and yet they glory in their shame."[10] Despite their appearance, another Union soldier commented. "Boys, he's not much for looks, but if we had him, we wouldn't have been caught in this trap."[11] Soldiers in the 3rd MD PHB infantry who were taken prisoner were paroled the next day and marched to Annapolis, MD to wait to be exchanged for Confederate prisoners of war. Most were released in June 1863.

POW record of Nathan P. R. Smith, who lived on a farm near Robinsonville in Monroe Township prior to volunteering in the 3rd MD PHB Infantry.[12]

Gettysburg - July 1st - 3rd, 1863

Bodies of Union soldiers, killed on July 1st, near the McPherson woods.

Confederate dead gathered for burial at the edge of the Rose woods on July 5.

Gettysburg Overview

The tide of war was favoring the Confederates as they marched North in June 1863. Robert E Lee had racked up impressive battlefield victories over the previous 12 months against four different Union Commanders. For the second time in as many years, Pennsylvania was being threatened by a major invasion of the Rebel army. Governor Curtin made an urgent call for 50,000 volunteers to join emergency militias to help defend Pennsylvania. Fear spread throughout the commonwealth when Lee's army crossed into Pennsylvania during the last week of June.

On July 1st, 1863, a division of Confederate Infantry ran into a Union Cavalry unit just west of Gettysburg. The fighting quickly escalated as soldiers from the invading Confederate army approached from the West and North as nearby Union army troops converged on the town from the South. By late afternoon, 30,000 Confederates had overwhelmed the 20,000 Union troops positioned on the hills and wooded areas just west and north of the town. But the heroic efforts of these outnumbered soldiers enabled the Union Army to seize defensible positions on the high ground around Gettysburg. On the afternoon of the second day, 90,000 Union troops successfully defended a 5-mile-long battle line against 71,000 Confederates during horrific fighting. Early in the afternoon of the third day, the Confederates unleashed a tremendous artillery bombardment on the center of the Union Army line before over 11,000 Confederates emerged from a wood line on Seminary Ridge and marched across on open field toward Cemetery Ridge. A few Confederate soldiers briefly breached the Union line at the Bloody Angle before the attack collapsed. Pickets Charge was a disaster for the Confederates, who lost approximately half their attacking force during the assault. The Confederacy's best chance to prevail in the war evaporated as surviving stragglers of this charge streamed back to Seminary Ridge.

The following evening, a demoralized Southern army retreated toward Virginia in a driving rainstorm, officially ending the bloodiest battle of the war. Northern troops suffered 23,000 casualties, including 3,100 soldiers who lost their lives. The Confederate Army suffered 28,000 casualties, including 3,900 who died during the 3-day battle. The 51,000 casualties suffered by both armies were by far the most of any single battle during the Civil War.[1]

There are 25 known Bedford County men and boys who were casualties during the Gettysburg campaign. Two of the wounded soldiers were 14 years old when they mustered in the army. Four members of the Gracey family, a father and 3 sons, volunteered in the 107th PA Infantry in 1862. During the 1st day of fighting, William Gracey suffered a neck wound and two of his sons, Alfred and James, were taken prisoner. Tragically, both sons spent the next 20 months in hellish Confederate prison camps, including the notorious Andersonville. Four Bedford County citizen soldiers never returned home. Others returned with ruined health or with wounds they would suffer from the rest of their lives.

This book does not cover the regimental locations of the following known casualties at Gettysburg. Levi Potter of the 56th PA Regiment suffered a wound during the 1st day of Gettysburg. The 56th PA was one of the first infantry regiments to be rushed to the Oak Ridge/Shead's Woods area of the battlefield on the morning of July 1st. Americus Enfield of Knap's Light Artillery was wounded on the 2nd Day of the battle near Culp's Hill. A third Union soldier, Emanuel Moses of the 18th PA Cavalry, was taken prisoner near Hagerstown on July 6th while pursuing the retreating rebel army. He later died of pneumonia at a Richmond POW camp on November 18th, 1864. One casualty was a Confederate soldier who moved to Bedford County after the war. Thomas J. Rollins was born in Spartanburg, SC and listed on the 1850 Spartanburg Census. Records show Thomas was taken prisoner at Gettysburg on July 3rd. The details of his capture are not known. His regiment, the 60th Georgia Infantry, took part in the evening assault on Cemetery Hill on July 2nd. Since his brigade was listed as occupying a position at the foot of Cemetery Ridge with only skirmishing reported between sharpshooters on July 3rd, it appears more likely he was captured during the assault on Cemetery Hill on the 2nd. Thomas was released from a POW camp in Louisville, Kentucky on June 8th, 1864 on the condition he remain North of the Ohio River. Thomas eventually ended up in Bedford County.[2]

Gettysburg - known Bedford Co. Casualty listing

Name	Muster Age	Rank	State	Regiment	Company	Casualty	Casualty Date
Enfield, Americus	14		PA	Knap's Light Art.	E	Wounded	7/2/63
Fessler, John B		Pvt.	PA	151st Infantry	H	Wounded	7/1/63
Foor, Jonathan S	22	Pvt.	PA	107th Infantry	H	POW	7/1/63
Gates, Martin	22	Pvt.	PA	110th Infantry	C	Wounded	7/2/63
Gracey, Alfred	18	Sgt.	PA	107th Infantry	H	POW	7/1/63
Gracey, James A	21	Pvt.	PA	107th Infantry	H	POW	7/1/63
Gracey, William C	42	1st Lt.	PA	107th Infantry	H	Wounded	7/1/63
Hammer, Joseph D		Pvt.	PA	142nd Infantry	D	Wound.-Died	7/1/63
Hays, Alexander Y	17	Pvt.	PA	110th Infantry	C	Wounded	7/2/63
Hixon, Henry H	21	Pvt.	PA	11th Infantry	A	Wound.-POW	7/1/63
Holsinger, Josiah	19	Pvt.	PA	110th Infantry	C	Wounded	7/2/63
Humbert, Wesley C	19	Corp.	PA	142nd Infantry	C	Wounded	7/1/63
Lamison, George W	23	Pvt.	PA	110th Infantry	C	Wound.-Died	7/2/63
Lohr, Benjamin F	20	Pvt.	PA	142nd Infantry	D	POW	7/1/63
Miller, John I	14	Pvt.	PA	110th Infantry	C	Wounded	7/2/63
Moore, John B	18	Sgt.	PA	110th Infantry	C	Wound.-POW	7/2/63
Moses, Emanuel	17	Pvt.	PA	18th Cavalry	K	POW-Died	7/6/63
Pee, Frances W	21	Sgt.	PA	11th Infantry	A	Wound.-POW	7/1/63
Potter, Levi	23	Pvt.	PA	56th Infantry	A	Wounded	7/1/63
Querry, Matthias	26	Pvt.	PA	53rd Infantry	C	Wounded	7/2/63*
Rollins, Thomas J	29	Pvt.	GA	60th Infantry	K	POW	7/3/63*
Sparks, Uriah	24	Sgt.	PA	107th Infantry	H	Wounded	7/1/63
Steinman, Mathew C	23	Pvt.	PA	62nd Infantry	M	Wounded	7/2/63
Tobias, Samuel H G	19	1st Sgt.	PA	110th Infantry	C	KIA	7/2/63
VanOrmer, William	20	Capt.	PA	53rd Infantry	I	Wounded	7/2/63

Above is an exceedingly rare photograph taken in the spring of 1863 of a known regimental company. The 110th PA Regiment, Company C was in heavy combat near the Wheatfield on the 2nd day at Gettysburg. Most soldiers in this company were from Morrisons Cove, including Woodbury and Loysburg. The names of these soldiers are not known.

Gettysburg Map

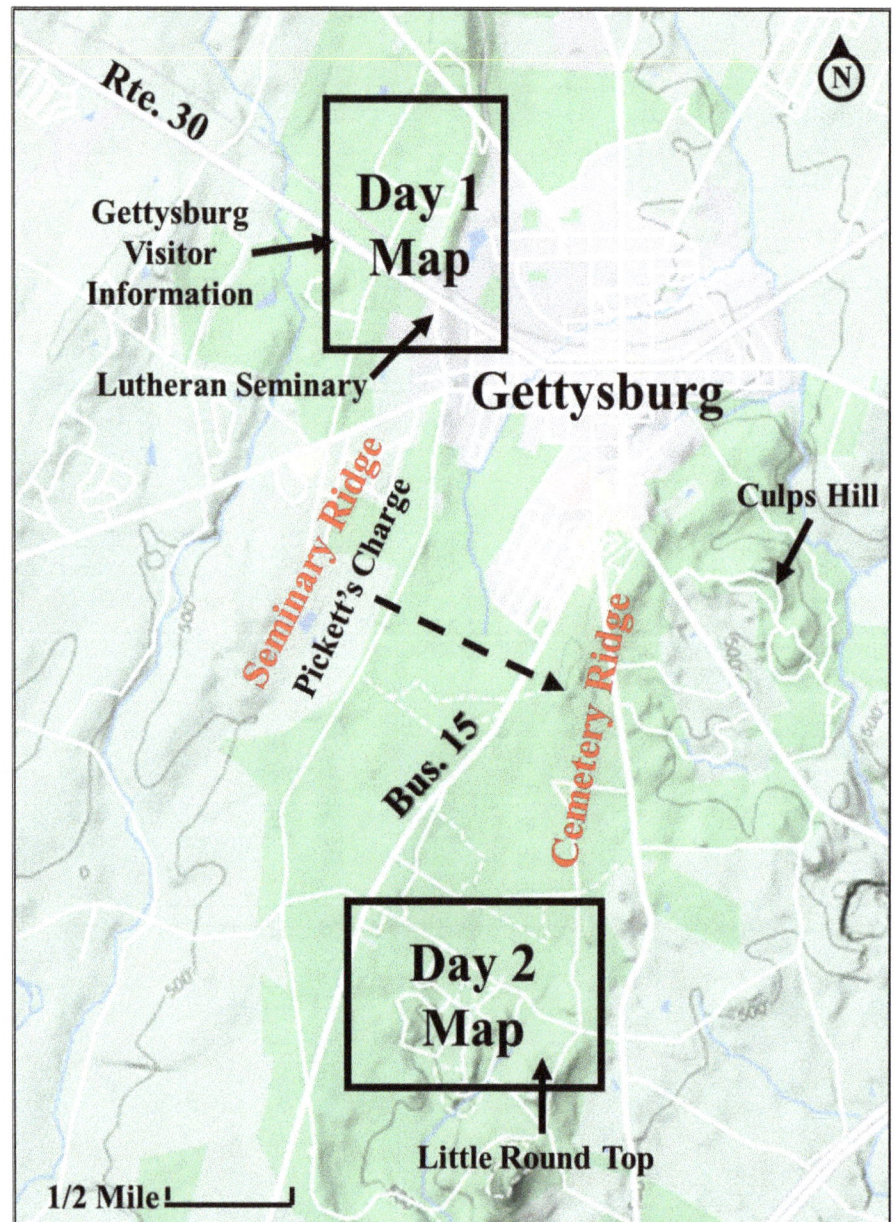

Bedford County casualties were suffered on the 1st and 2nd days of the 3-day battle. Most county soldiers were in support or reserve assignments near Cemetery Ridge during Pickett's Charge on the 3rd day. Location maps for both Day 1 and Day 2 for the regiments that suffered multiple Bedford County casualties are on the following pages.

The invading rebel army drove outnumbered Union soldiers from their positions just west and north of the town at the end of the 1st day of the battle. During the next two days, the Confederates occupied Seminary Ridge while the Union lines stretched 5 miles along Cemetery Ridge from Culps Hill to Little Round Top. On the 2nd day of the battle, the rebel army launched major assaults on the left flank of the Union army at Little Round Top and the Wheatfield areas of the battlefield and on the Union right at Culp's Hill. After these assaults were repulsed, Robert E. Lee ordered Confederate troops massed along Seminary Ridge to attack the middle of the Union lines on the afternoon of the 3rd day of the battle. Pickett's Charge ended in disaster for the rebel army.

The Bedford County tour of the battlefield will start at the Gettysburg Visitors Information building on the right side of the road on Rte. 30 just as you enter the Gettysburg National Park.

As you approach Gettysburg from the west, pull into the Gettysburg Visitor Information building and walk to the top of the hill to gain a good perspective of the battlefield on Day 1.

Bedford County soldiers in the 11th PA and 107th PA regiments fought in and around Shead's Woods. County soldiers in the 142nd were in the field in front of the Lutheran Seminary.

Photo circa 1890 of the Chambersburg Pike (Route 30) looking east toward Seminary Ridge.

Day 1 Map

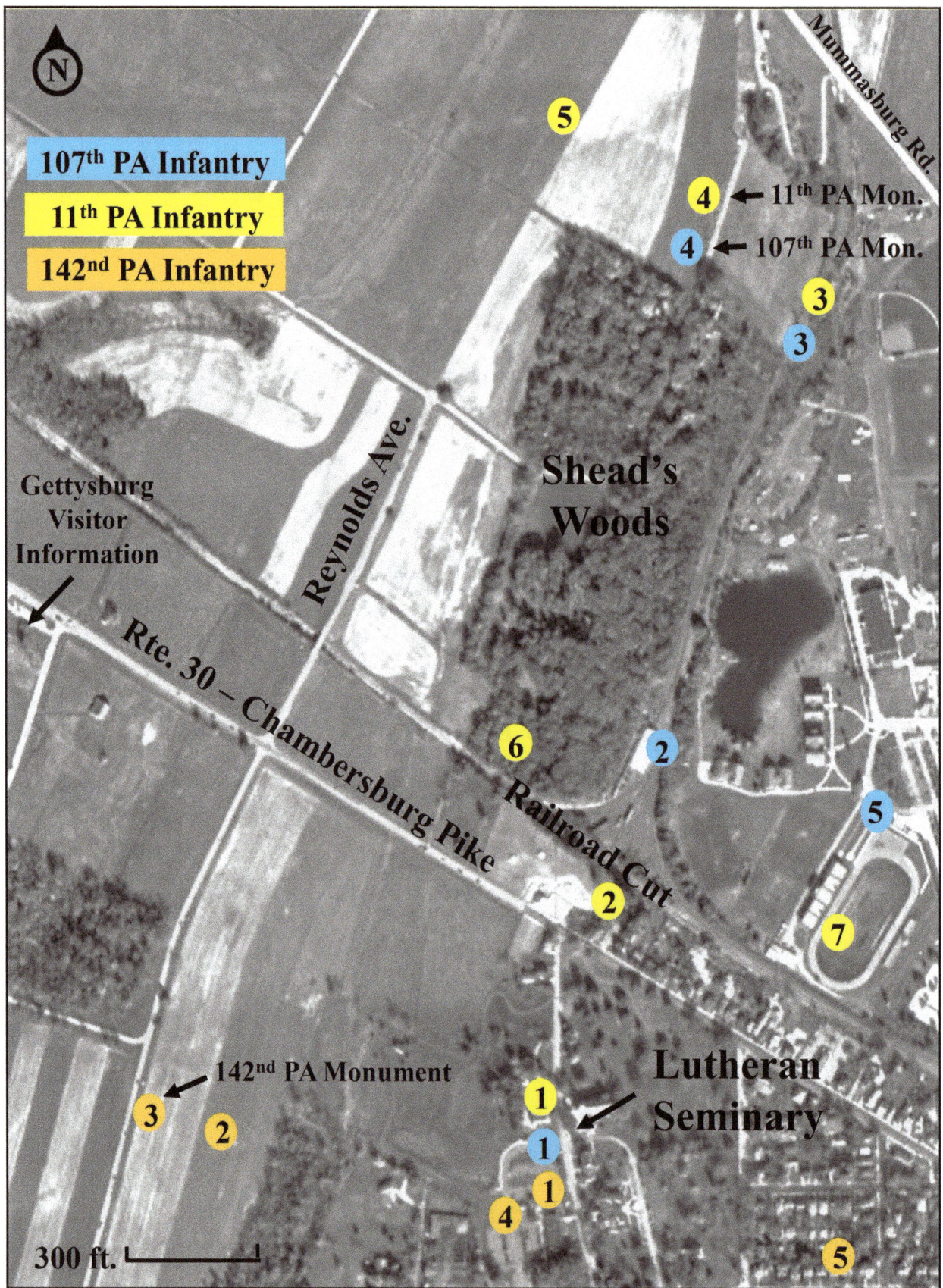

Day 1 of the Gettysburg battle driving directions:

Right out of the parking lot of the Gettysburg Visitor Information on to Rte. 30 & proceed 0.4 miles to the top of the hill.

Right on Seminary Ridge Road. The Lutheran Seminary will be on the left in 0.2 miles. Pull into the parking lot on the right directly across from the Lutheran Seminary.

The 1st Corps of the Union Army, including 11th, 107th and 142nd Pennsylvania Regiments, marched north from the Pennsylvania-Maryland border early in the morning of July 1st. Around 9:30 am, the first regiments of the 1st Corps reached the Lutheran Seminary and were forming battle lines in the fields on both sides of Rte. 30 (referred to as the Chambersburg Pike during the Civil War). The 11th and 107th PA Regiments were approximately 3 miles south of Gettysburg on the Emmitsburg Road (Bus. Rte. 15) near Big Roundtop when they first heard rifle fire between Union Cavalry and Confederate Infantry units. The 11th and the 107th PA regiments exited the Emmitsburg Road and pushed forward over fields to the west of the road, bypassing the town of Gettysburg. Around 11:00 am, the 11th and 107th arrived at the Lutheran Seminary and began erecting trenches just down the hill from the Seminary.[3]

- **(2)** By noon, the 11th PA advanced across the Chambersburg Pike to a position just south of the Railroad Cut. The 11th PA briefly halted at this location before being rushed to fill a gap in the Union lines. The
- **(3)** 11th PA proceeded across the Railroad Cut and moved forward about a quarter of a mile along the foot of Oak Ridge, past the northern edge of Shead's Woods.[4]
- **(2)** Around noon, the 142nd PA advanced across the above field below the Lutheran Seminary in the above 1863 photograph. The 142nd PA held the position shown on the map on the left during the next 3 hours of the battle.[5]

Exit the parking lot.

Left on Seminary Ridge Road & return to Rte. 30.

Left on Rte. 30 & proceed 0.2 miles.

Right at Reynolds Avenue and proceed across a small bridge in about 400 feet. Park on the right side of the road after crossing the bridge.

Photograph of the railroad cut in 1886. Shead's Woods is to the left of the cut in the distance. During the battle, this railroad cut was unfinished without rail tracks and was only 3 to 4 feet in depth in most places. Shead's Woods sits on Oak Ridge. Both names are referred to on Civil War documents. The 11th and 107th PA Regiments were positioned in the clearing just to the left of Shead's Woods. Later in the afternoon, the 11th PA shifted into Shead's Woods close to the railroad cut. Please note this photograph shows the woods during the Civil War era were not as thick as today. A Gettysburg Park Ranger stated prior to the battle, local livestock grazed in and around many of the wooded areas surrounding Gettysburg and there would have been less undergrowth among the groves of trees than is visible in the park today.

Proceed 0.1 miles to Buford Ave. & take a Left.

Proceed 0.6 miles & take a Right at the 1st stop sign.

Proceed 0.2 miles & take a Right at the Observation Tower.

Park in the Observation Tower parking lot. The Observation Tower on Doubleday Avenue provides a superb view of the battlefield.

Proceed 0.1 miles to the 107th and 11th PA monuments & pull over on the Right side of the road near the monuments.

The above photograph was taken from the observation tower on Doubleday Avenue. The monuments of the 11th and 107th PA regiments are at the end of the road in the photo. Shead's Woods is in the background. Both the 11th and the 107th charged up the hill on the left to the crest of Oak Ridge and took positions on the Union line near the stone wall on the left side of the road. The stone wall was bitterly fought over during multiple Confederate assaults on the afternoon of July 1st. The sloping terrain hid soldiers from view on both sides of the stone wall, resulting in devastating close contact rifle fire during the battle.

On the left is one of the most well-known monuments in Gettysburg. In the center of the 11th Pennsylvania monument on the bottom pedestal lays a likeness of their beloved mascot, "Sallie," The following is a verbatim excerpt from the Gettysburgsculptures.com website. "Sallie would be given to the members of the regiment when only a puppy. She would serve with the men in the ranks and suffer the hardships of long campaigns as well as the victories won on many fields. It was reported Sallie would be seen in the ranks and in line of battle, barking as bullets whizzed by her. At Gettysburg, she became separated from her friends of the 11th during their retreat through town. Not sure of where to go, she would return to the battle line of the first day's battle and would be found several days later resting among the dead and wounded until she rejoined her comrades of the 11th. Sallie would serve with the 11th until she was killed during the battle of Hatcher's Run, Virginia, on February 6, 1865. Today she is remembered on the western face of the monument, as she calmly looks across the fields of Gettysburg in search of her old friends."

Uriah Sparks was 19 years old when he left his home in Hopewell to enlist as a sergeant in the 107th PA Infantry in 1862. He was wounded during desperate fighting on the 1st Day of the battle of Gettysburg. Uriah passed in 1893 and is buried at the Providence Union Cemetery in Everett.[6]

Joseph Armstrong was a 1st Lt. in the 11th PA Infantry at Gettysburg, while his wife Anna was at home with 5 small children in Hopewell Township. In a letter to his wife, Joseph wrote "Keep my little ones well… for I never expect to see them again in this world." Joseph received a disability discharge and was able to see his wife and children before passing after returning home shortly after the war ended.[7]

At around 12:30, the 11th PA reached the stone wall at the top of Oak Ridge to fill a gap in the Union line as Confederate Col. Edward O'Neal's Alabama regiments attack the Union line north of Shead's Woods. Multiple Confederate assaults were repulsed.[8]

William Henry Locke, a veteran of the 11th PA Infantry, recalled, "the battle grew fiercer with every hour. Gallantly the rebels came against our front, and as gallantly they were driven back. **"We are Pennsylvanians and have come here to stay"** was shouted by soldiers in the 11th PA following every repulse of the enemy. There seemed to be no end to those Southern ranks, as there was no exhausting the persistent courage with which they continued the attack. Quick as one line was swept away, another and a stronger line took its place." [9]

Around 2:30, Confederate Gen. Alfred Iverson's North Carolina regiments advanced across the open field in front of the stone wall while Union regiments remain hidden from view. One soldier a couple hundred yards down the Union line from the 11th PA recalled, "Iverson confidently marched to the attack with a line as straight as if on parade, apparently unaware of the hostile troops crouching in the shadow of the low stone wall in his front. When the Carolinians were about 100 paces distant, men arose and poured a withering fire into their faces with terrible effect. Hundreds of the Confederates fell at the first volley, plainly marking their line with a ghastly row of dead and wounded men, whose blood trailed the course of their line with a crimson stain clearly discernible for several days after the battle, until the rain washed the gory record away. Those who were uninjured broke to the rear, taking refuge from the pitiless storm in a little gully or depression about 200 paces from the Union line." While Iverson's regiments are engulfed in defenseless confusion, the 11th PA and other Union regiments climbed over the stone wall and launched a counter-charge, capturing 500 rebel prisoners.[10]

Shortly before 3:00, the 107th PA and four other Union regiments were rushed from below the Lutheran Seminary toward the Union line north of Shead's Woods. The 11th PA and five other regiments who were defending the Union line at the stone wall prepare to shift to new positions in Shead's Woods and are running desperately low in ammunition.[11] The spirited and determined heroics of the outnumbered Union soldiers fighting on their home soil for the first time are under extreme pressure from recently arrived rebel troops being thrown at them.

Alfred Gracey left his East Providence Township home with his father William and two brothers to volunteer in the 107th PA Infantry. During the first day at Gettysburg, Alfred and his brother James were taken prisoner. Both survived 20 months of captivity in POW camps. Albert was so weak, he needed to be carried from the Andersonville POW camp to board the train home. It took him a year of rest and medical care to recover.[12]

Alfred's younger brother, George Gracey, was 16 when he volunteered in the 107th PA with his father and brothers in 1862. George was the only member of his family who was not a battlefield casualty on July 1st. All four members of the family survived the war and returned home to Bedford County.[13]

④ Around 3:45 Confederate Gen. Junius Daniel's North Carolina and Alabama regiments mount an assault on the entire Union line along Oak Ridge. The initial Confederate charge is repulsed, but Union General Gabriel Paul suffers a horrific wound that scribed a path through both eyes, blinding him. Because of the intensity of the fighting and confusion in the ranks, command of the Union brigade north of Shead's Woods gets passed to 3 different Colonels in a matter of minutes.[14]

Photograph of the 107th PA monument from behind the stone wall, looking across the field where county soldiers turned back multiple Rebel army assaults on July 1st.

Proceed 0.2 miles on Doubleday Avenue.

Left at Reynolds Avenue.

Proceed 0.2 miles & take Left at the next traffic signal onto Rte. 30.

Proceed 0.2 miles & take Right at the top of the hill on Seminary Ridge.

Proceed 0.3 miles past the Lutheran Seminary & take a right on Middle Street at the next traffic Signal.

Proceed 0.4 miles & turn Right on Reynolds Ave. just after the small Auto Tour Sign.

Proceed 0.4 miles to the 142nd PA Monument (photographed below) on the right.

② The 142nd PA advance to a position west of their monument, near the Herbst Woods, around noon. At 3:30, North Confederate regiments under Gen. James Pettigrew launch an assault that drives back the Union regiments on both flanks of the 142nd.[15]

③ The 142nd makes a heroic counter-charge as other Union regiments around them begin to retreat. They push back the Confederate advance in front of them and hold a position near their monument for a brief time before being forced to withdrawal. Col. Robert Cummins of the 142nd is mortally wounded during the withdrawal.[16]

④ By 4:00, the entire Union line on this side of the Chambersburg Pike (Rte. 30) has been pushed back to a position within 100 yards of the Lutheran Seminary.[17]

Benjamin Lohr is pictured with his son after the war. Benjamin volunteered in the 142nd PA Regiment in 1862 and was captured on the 1st day at Gettysburg. After being released 4 months later, Benjamin was deemed physically unable to continue his enlistment because of the harsh living conditions at the POW camp. Benjamin married after the war and raised 10 children. He was listed as a farmer on the 1880 East St. Clair Twp. Census. Benjamin lived to be 80 years old and is buried in the Grandview Cemetery in Cambria County.[18]

1863 photograph of the town of Gettysburg taken from Seminary Ridge shortly after the battle.

By 4:00 pm, the entire Union army line begins to buckle from a devastating coordinated Confederate assault reinforced with recently arrived troops. With no other Union troops nearby to throw at the rebel invaders, a retreat was ordered through the town of Gettysburg to Cemetery Hill. The chaotic retreat through the town was described in the 11th PA Regiment history book, "It was a sight never to be forgotten. Crowding through the streets, and up the alleys, and over fences in utter ignorance of whither they were going, every moment increased the confusion and dismay. To add to the terrors of the hour, the enemy gained possession of the town, and firing rapidly into our retreating ranks, shot and shell mingled their horrid sounds with the groans of the dying thus stricken down." [19] The remaining Union soldiers who were not killed, wounded, or captured feverishly formed a new battle line along Cemetery Ridge to prepare for another Rebel assault they knew was coming.

Day 2 of the Gettysburg battle driving directions:

From 142nd Monument proceed forward 0.2 miles and take a Right on Rte. 30.

Proceed 0.7 miles & veer left at the 1st traffic signal onto Chambersburg St.

Proceed 0.2 miles & take a Right at the traffic circle onto Bus. Rte. 15 / Baltimore St.

Proceed 0.4 miles & take a Right at the Steinwehr Ave. traffic signal onto Bus. Rte. 15.

Proceed for 2.1 miles to an UNMARKED GRAVEL LANE (after passing Millerstown Road, proceed to the top of the next hill to the Unmarked Gravel Lane).

Left on the UNMARKED GRAVEL LANE.

Rose House property will be at the end of the gravel lane.
The Rose House property is owned by the National Park Service.

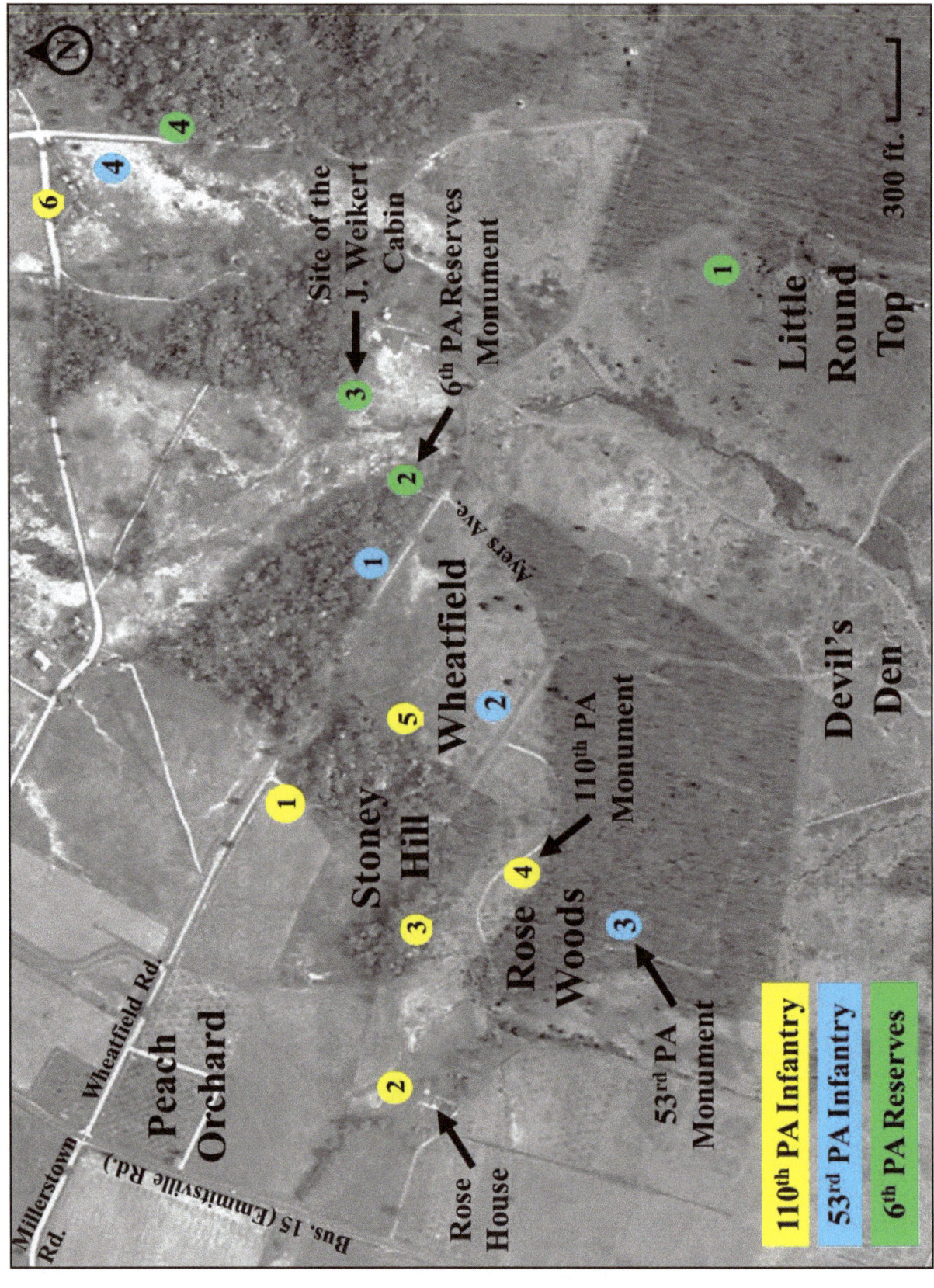

Between the outbuildings of the Rose House is a view of the southwest corner of the Wheatfield.

Left of the Rose House along a fence affords a view of the battlefield locations you will be visiting. Bedford County soldiers in the 110th PA were located near the north side of the Rose House from about 2:00 p.m. until around 3:30 on July 2nd, when the regiment shifted to a position at the foot of Stoney Hill.

After parking near the Rose House, walk to the north side of the Rose House property for a good perspective of the locations of Bedford County soldiers during the 2nd Day at Gettysburg, as shown on the photographs on the right.

On the 2nd day of the battle, Bedford County soldiers in the 110th PA Regiment marched north from the Pennsylvania-Maryland border on the Emmitsburg Pike (Business Rte. 15) past the Rose House gravel lane you just turned on and took a right at the Peach Orchard onto Wheatfield Road and formed a battle-line near Stoney Hill around 1:00 p.m.

James Hamilton of the 110th PA later wrote of his observations of local citizens as they turned off the Emmitsburg Pike (Business Rte. 15) onto Wheatfield Road. "As we turned the corner a host of the gentry of the country, in all sorts of dress, from the fine silk hat to the roughest homespun, riding all kinds of animals, from the nondescript plug to the most fiery steed, came into the Peach Orchard. They, no doubt, had come to see a battle, and were anxious to get a view of the rebels. Their number and our appearance at the same time attracted the attention of a rebel battery that had a good range, and soon the shells commenced to drop among them, burst overhead and all around them. In a twinkling the horses were rearing and plunging, hats flying, riders tumbling with eyes sticking out of their heads. Amidst the most unearthly yelling, the horses ran in one direction while their riders went another. I do not know whether any of them were killed or not. We were not anxious to wait and see." [20]

Return to Bus. Rte. 15 & take a Right.

Proceed 0.2 miles & take Right at the intersection on Millerstown Rd. / Wheatfield Rd.

Proceed 0.6 miles & take a Right at Ayers Ave and immediately park the car on the right side of the road.

James Levi Roush

To the left of your parked car, you will see a view of Little Round Top similar to the above photograph taken shortly after the battle. Big Round Top is on the far right of this picture. The 6th PA Reserves reached the east side of Little Round Top on the afternoon of July 2nd, 1863. They observed Union lines near Devil's Den and the Wheatfield being driven back by the Rebel army. The 6th PA Reserves rushed down the slope of Little Round Top toward the current location of the 6th Reserve Monument.

Directly to the rear of your parked car on the corner of Wheatfield Rd. and Ayers Ave. is an opening in the rail fence across Wheatfield Road, as shown in the photographs below.

Walk 50 yards down the unmarked path in the above photographs to the 6th PA Reserves monument.

James Levi Roush was one of only 64 Union soldiers awarded the Medal of Honor at Gettysburg. James was born near the Bedford-Blair County line in 1838. He left his home near Sarah Furnace to volunteer in the 6th PA Reserves in 1861. James was shot in the face during the 2nd Battle of Bull Run but recovered and rejoined his regiment. On the 2nd Day of Gettysburg, Confederate sharpshooters were targeting Union soldiers from the J. Weikert cabin (no longer standing). While under heavy fire, James and 5 other men charged the cabin and captured all 12 Confederate sharpshooters. James mustered out of the army in June 1864. He married in 1865 and was a father to 8 children. James passed at age 68 and is buried at the new St. Patrick's Cemetery in Newry.[21]

Continue 0.2 miles on Ayers Ave to 1st stop sign & proceed straight.

Proceed 0.4 miles & the 53rd PA Monument will be on the right side of the road.

(Left) is the 53rd PA Regiment monument.

(Right) William W VanOrmer was 20 years old when he mustered as a 1st Sergeant in the 53rd PA Infantry in 1861. He was wounded three times during the Civil War. William suffered a wound at Antietam in September 1862, at Gettysburg on July 2nd and at Spotsylvania in May 1864. During the war, he received three promotions and mustered out as a Captain on June 30th, 1865. He married in 1868 and was a father of 6 children. William lived to be 81 years old and is buried in the Schellsburg Cemetery.[22]

1. Between 3:00 and 4:00 pm, the 53rd PA Regiment formed a battle line behind the northeastern edge of the Wheatfield. The 53rd rushed into the middle of the Wheatfield around 6:30 and exchanged rifle fire with soldiers in Georgia and South Carolina regiments. While also under rebel artillery fire, the 53rd
2. PA fixed bayonets and charged toward the bottom of the hill at the Wheatfield, driving back Confederates and taking prisoners. The 53rd PA continued their charge through the Rose Woods and reached a
3. position near their monument. This forward position was held for a short time. Rebel troops mounted a counter-charge and flanked Union regiments on both sides of the 53rd. Shortly before 7:15 pm, the 53rd PA fell back through the Wheatfield under heavy fire to a site northeast of the Wheatfield.[23]

Proceed 0.2 miles on Brooke Ave. which will turn into DeTrobriand Ave. The 110th PA Monument is on the right. Pull over near the monument.

The bronze soldier on top of the monument of the 110th Pennsylvania Regiment is facing the Rose Woods, where the 8th and 9th Georgia Infantry regiments launched assaults on the afternoon of July 2nd. Around 4:00, the 110th defended a position at the foot of Stoney Hill close to a ravine at the location indicated in the above photograph. James Hamilton, a sergeant in the 110th, later wrote, "Scarcely had we got into position when we heard the fearful rebel yell. On they came like an avalanche. A herd of cattle, pasturing in the woods, rushed madly down in front of their line. Nearly the entire herd fell at the first fire. On came the enemy, nearer, but slowly, a step at a time. The Rebels met a living wall and could not pass it. My friend Samuel Tobias (from Bedford County) died at my side and many others were killed." [24] Col. DeTrobriand wrote in his memoir, "The Confederates appeared to have the devil in them. When the Rebels descended in the ravine and crossed the creek, they were received, at a distance of twenty yards, with a deadly volley, every shot of which was effective. On both sides, each aimed at targets and men fell dead and wounded with frightful rapidity." [25] Late in the afternoon, the 110th shifted from the foot of Stoney Hill to a position near the 110th Monument to fill a gap in the Union line. Around 5:45, with ammunition running low, the entire Union line below the Wheatfield fell back. Hamilton recalled, "We had a few moments to breathe and look at the scene of desolation. The sun was scorching hot. The tide of battle swept to the rear, the right, and to the left. The acting adjutant rushed to the top of the bluff, saw the enemy wrapping up to the left and at the foot of Little Round Top. The adjutant reported what he had seen to Major Isaac Rodgers. Rodgers immediately shouted, "About face" and "Double quick!" We climbed the bluff and made our way back through the Wheatfield across the road." [26]

The mangled body of Confederate soldier near the tree line at the Rose Woods

Benjamin Shoemaker and his brother Austin left their Middle Woodbury Twp. home to volunteer in the 110th PA Infantry in 1861. Both brothers fought together at Gettysburg. Benjamin married after the war and was a father of 2 children. He passed in 1929 and is buried at the Holsinger Cemetery in Bakers Summit.[27]

John I. Miller (right) was 14 years old when he left his Morrisons Cove home to volunteer in the 110th Pennsylvania Infantry on December 19, 1861. He suffered a face wound during the 2nd day of Gettysburg near the Rose Woods at the foot of the Wheatfield. John recovered from his wound and mustered out of the army on April 10th, 1864. He married after the war and raised a family. John passed at age 48 on March 6th, 1896. He is buried in the Bedford Cemetery.[28]

John S. Border was born in Schellsburg in 1841. He left his Woodbury home to join the 110th PA in 1861. John received a head wound at the battle of Kelly's Ford in March 1863. He recovered and was injured a month later at Chancellorsville, when his foot was run over by a cannon wheel. John was captured but was able to slip away from his captors while marching to a POW camp. He rejoined the 110th PA and fought at Gettysburg.[29]

Thomas G. Livingston was born in Hopewell in 1837. He mustered in the 110th PA in 1861. A Minie ball passed through his hip and back during hand-to-hand combat at Spotsylvania in 1864. Thomas recovered and was promoted to 1st Sgt. He was promoted a second time to 2nd Lt. just before the war ended. Thomas returned home and was a father to 6 children. Thomas passed at age 70 and is buried at the Everett Cemetery.[30]

Proceed 0.1 miles on DeTrobriand Ave. & pull over just prior to reaching the stop sign.
About 40 yards to the right is the "The Bloody Wheatfield marker." From the marker, a mowed path extends to the 1st NY Artillery Monument.

The above photograph of the Wheatfield shows the locations of the 110th PA Regiment counter-charge and where the 53rd PA Regiment drove Rebel soldiers from their position at the bottom of the hill.

After being driven back, the 110th mounted a counter-charge against Georgia regiments between the 1st NY Artillery Monument and tree line in the above photograph before withdrawing from the battle.

    Col. DeTrobriand wrote the following in a memoir, "The enemy, profiting by our movement in retreat, advanced into the Wheatfield, on the edge of which I rallied what remained of the 5th Michigan and 110th PA and we charged through the Wheatfield, driving the rebels back to the other side of the stone wall. It was the first charge of the day on the ground, which saw so many more before night." [31]

Before continuing on, take time to reflect on the recollections of a soldier on the chaotic whirlwind that overwhelmed the senses of all who were at the Wheatfield on July 2nd, 1863, "Generals, colonels, aids, and orderlies galloped about through the smoke while hoarse and indistinguishable orders were being shouted by commanding officers; The screaming and bursting of shells, cannister, and shrapnel created a swishing sound as they tore through the struggling masses of humanity; The death screams of animals and the groans of their wounded and dying human companions commingled while both man and beast were being trampled underfoot by hurrying batteries; Riderless horses and the moving lines of battle all combined into an indescribable roar of discordant elements. It was a perfect hell on earth, never perhaps to be equaled, certainly not to be surpassed, nor ever to be forgotten in a man's lifetime. It is never erased from my memory, day or night, for 50 years." [32]

Proceed to the stop sign & take a left.

Proceed up Stoney Hill approximately 0.1 mile from the stop sign. The road will veer sharply to the right & the field where the 110th PA was positioned will be on the left as shown in the photograph below.

Nearly 35% of the soldiers in the 110th PA on the battlefield were killed, wounded, or captured during two hours of combat. The Union regiment located next to the 110th PA, the 5th Michigan, suffered over 50% casualties. During the dedication of the 110th PA Monument at Gettysburg in 1889, a veteran stated, "the 110th PA Regiment was not driven from its position in front of Stoney Hill; it withdrew to the Wheatfield only after the Union line of battle had been pierced on both sides of the regiment." [33]

Continue 0.1 miles to a stop sign & take a right on Wheatfield Rd.

Proceed 0.6 miles & take a left on Sedgwick Ave.

Proceed 0.8 miles on Sedgwick Ave. which turns into Hancock Ave. and the State of Pennsylvania Monument will be on your right.

Pennsylvania Monument at Gettysburg

The State of Pennsylvania Monument was dedicated in 1910 and is the largest monument on the Gettysburg battlefield. The monument is 110 feet high at the top of the Winged Victory statue. The roof of the monument offers visitors a panoramic view of the battlefield. The monument is lined with bronze tablets of the Pennsylvania regiments and batteries who fought at Gettysburg. Each tablet lists the regimental roster by company. The monument has the names of over 34,000 Pennsylvanians who took part in the battle.

The inscription at the front entrance states Pennsylvania contributed...
69 Regiments Infantry
9 Regiments Cavalry
7 Batteries Artillery
34,530 Soldiers present
1,182 Killed and mortally wounded
3,177 Wounded
860 Missing

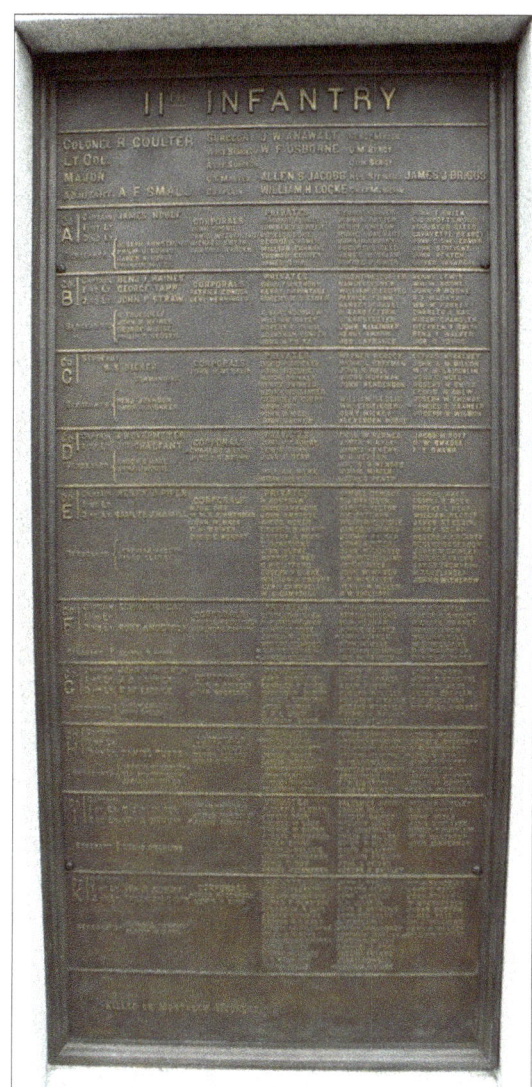

(top left) Gettysburg veterans reading the bronze tablets during the 50th anniversary of the battle in July 1913. (top right) 11th Pennsylvania Infantry bronze tablet. (bottom) Bedford County soldiers in the 11th PA Infantry, Company A who fought at Gettysburg are listed.

Bedford County veterans and their monuments

18th PA Cavalry Monument is near where their charge was made at the foot of Big Roundtop on July 3rd.

Knap's Independent Light Artillery Monument on Culp's Hill. Americus Enfield was wounded near here on July 2nd while dueling with Confederate artillery units on Benner's Hill.

William Nelson was born in 1847. William was 15 years old when he mustered as a corporal in the 18th PA Cavalry in November 1862. His father John mustered as a 1st Lieutenant in the same cavalry unit a month later. John was shot in the shoulder and hip while skirmishing with Mosby's Raiders, an infamous Confederate guerilla unit near Chantilly, Virginia, on February 26th, 1863. The wound required amputation of his right leg at the hip. William remained in the 18th PA Cavalry and fought at Gettysburg. He mustered out after the war and returned home to help his father run the family flour mill. William moved to Southern California after retiring. He passed at age 70 in 1917.[34]

Americus Enfield was born in 1847. Americus was 14 years old when he mustered in Knap's Independent Light Artillery, Battery E in June 1861. He was wounded on the 2nd Day of Gettysburg near Culp's Hill. Americus re-enlisted as a surgeon in the 22nd PA Cavalry in February 1864. He married in 1870 and was a father to 6 children. Americus was a well-known Doctor in Bedford County after the war and can often be identified in Civil War veterans group pictures by his tall stature and prominent sideburns. He lived to be 83 years old and was buried in the Bedford Cemetery in 1931. Inscribed on his gravestone is "He lived for Humanity."[35]

(left) The wedding picture of William & Ann Lowery, in 1868. William mustered in the 18th PA Cavalry in 1862. He was captured at Germanna Ford and was a POW from November 1863 until April 1865. William and Ann were parents to 7 sons.[36]

(right) Benjamin Oliver left his home in Cumberland Valley to volunteer in the 18th PA Cavalry in 1862. He mustered out in October 1865. Benjamin passed in 1928 at age 80.[37]

(left) William Raley Albright was born in 1843 on a farm in Londonderry Township. William had a highly unusual wartime experience. He enlisted in both the Confederate and Union armies during the Civil War. William initially enlisted in the 114th Militia and in the 33rd Virginia Infantry under Stonewall Jackson. William deserted the Confederate army and volunteered in the 18th Pennsylvania Cavalry in November 1862. His was described at enlistment as a 19-year-old farmer, was 6' tall with dark hair, dark eyes, and a fair complexion. William enlisted under his mother's maiden name. The spelling of his last name on various Union Army records was Raily. There was a good reason for the name change. If William was captured and identified as a Confederate deserter, he likely would have been hung on the spot. Seven months after mustering in the Union Cavalry, the former Confederate was in combat at the battle of Gettysburg. A statue of the 18th PA Cavalry is near Big Round Top, where William took part in a charge on the afternoon of Picket's Charge. Below, William Raily's name is listed on the 18th PA Cavalry plaque on the Pennsylvania State Monument at Gettysburg, confirming he took part in the battle. He married after the war ended and raised 7 children on a family farm in Londonderry Township. William passed at age 69 in 1913.[38]

Gettysburg Address, November 19, 1863

Fourscore and seven years ago our fathers brought forth on this continent, a new nation, conceived in Liberty, and dedicated to the proposition that all men are created equal.

Now we are engaged in a great civil war, testing whether that nation, or any nation so conceived and so dedicated, can long endure. We are met on a great battle-field of that war. We have come to dedicate a portion of that field, as a final resting place for those who here gave their lives that that nation might live. It is altogether fitting and proper that we should do this.

But, in a larger sense, we can not dedicate-we can not consecrate-we can not hallow-this ground. The brave men, living and dead, who struggled here, have consecrated it, far above our poor power to add or detract. The world will little note, nor long remember what we say here, but it can never forget what they did here. It is for us the living, rather, to be dedicated here to the unfinished work which they who fought here have thus far so nobly advanced. It is rather for us to be here dedicated to the great task remaining before us-that from these honored dead we take increased devotion to that cause for which they gave the last full measure of devotion-that we here highly resolve that these dead shall not have died in vain-that this nation, under God, shall have a new birth of freedom-and that government of the people, by the people, for the people shall not perish from the earth.

Closeup of the only known photograph of Abraham Lincoln giving the Gettysburg Address.

Notes

1. Antietam Campaign

1. Gottfried, Bradley M. *The Maps of Antietam*, Savas Beatie, 2012, p.6.
2. Roadside marker at the Mountain House near Turner's Gap, 6132 Old National Pike, Boonsboro, MD.
3. Hoffsommer, Robert D. "Jackson's Capture of Harpers Ferry." *Civil War Times Illustrated.* August 1862, p.10.
4. Gottfried, *The Maps of Antietam*, p.18.
5. Nilsson, Jeff. "Mr. Lincoln Discusses His Proclamation," *The Saturday Evening Post,* 22 September 2012, https://www.saturdayeveningpost.com/2012/09/emancipation-proclamation/.

2. South Mountain

Enlistment, casualty, and other individual soldier details were sourced from my first book, Civil War Soldiers of Bedford County Pennsylvania.

Many resources contributed to the regimental locations shown on the battlefield map of South Mountain. These sources include the regimental history books, memoirs, official army records, newspaper articles, and the following two books.

Gottfried, Bradley M. *The Maps of Antietam*, Sevas Beatie, 2012.

Priest, John M. *Before Antietam: The Battle for South Mountain*, Oxford University Press, 1989.

1. Andrew J Foor photograph courtesy of ConnerFamilykkkk in *Ancestry.com*; biographical information sourced from *Ancestry.com*.
2. 1862 Painting of Union Troops charging Confederates holding the higher ground at Turner's Gap by H. Charles McBarron.
3. Eli Eichelberger photograph courtesy of Linda Bunch; biographical information sourced from *Ancestry.com*.
4. Lewis B Waltz photograph courtesy of Ronn Palm; biographical information sourced from *Ancestry.com*.
5. Photograph and Article courtesy of the *Bedford Gazette* (undated).
6. Locke, William Henry. *The Story of the Regiment*, Philadelphia, J.B. Lippincott & Co. 1868, p.121.
7. Holsinger, Frank. "South Mountain, and the Part of the Pennsylvania Reserves Took in the Battle." *The National Tribune*, 27 September 1883, p.7.
8. Hill, Ashbel, *Our boys. The personal experiences of a soldier in the Army of the Potomac*, Philadelphia, J.E. Potter Publishing, 1864, p.395.
9. Joseph Garber House photograph courtesy of Maryland Historical Trust State Historic Sites.
10. Holsinger. "South Mountain." *The National Tribune*, p.7.
11. Hill, *Our boys,* pp.395-396.
12. Park, Robert Emory, *Sketch of the Twelfth Alabama Infantry of Battle's Brigade*, Richmond, W.E. Jones Printer, 1906, p.88-89.
13. Park, *Sketch of the Twelfth Alabama* photograph.
14. Holsinger. "South Mountain." *The National Tribune*, p. 7.
15. Hill, *Our boys*, p.396.
16. Official Army Record, volume 19-chapter 31, #260, Col. F.W. McMaster (17th Carolina).
17. Official Army Record, volume 19-chapter 31, #28, Capt. James MacThomson (107th PA).
18. Jonathan S Foor photograph courtesy of Foor Family Military History Book; biographical information sourced from *Ancestry.com*
19. Official Army Record, volume 19-chapter 31, #36, Col. Albert Magilton (8th PA Res.)
20. Sypher, Josiah, *History of the Pennsylvania Reserve Corps,* Lancaster, PA, Elias Barr & Co. 1865, p. 370.
21. Hill, *Our boys*, p.397.
22. William H. Kay images and biographical information sourced on *Ancestry.com* and *Findagrave.com*.
23. Matthew P. Shaw diary image courtesy of the Bedford Historical Society, biographical information sourced from *Ancestry.com*.

3. Antietam

Enlistment, casualty, and other individual soldier details were sourced from my first book, Civil War Soldiers of Bedford County Pennsylvania.

Many resources contributed to the regimental locations shown on the battlefield maps of Antietam. These sources include the regimental history books, memoirs, official army records, newspaper articles, and the following two books.

Gottfried, Bradley M. *The Maps of Antietam*, Sevas Beatie, 2012.

Priest, John M. Antietam: *The Soldiers' Battle*, Oxford University Press, 1989.

1. Freeman, Ankrum, "Sidelights on Brethren History," *The Brethren Press*, 1962, pp. 109-116.
2. Hartwig, Scott. "The Maryland Campaign of 1862," *American Battlefield Trust*, (n.d.), https://www.battlefields.org/learn/articles/maryland-campaign-1862.
3. "Farming the Cornfield: D. R. Miller's 1862 Harvest of Death." *Antietam's Cornfield*, 18 Oct. 2017, https://antietamscornfield.com/2017/10/18/farming-the-cornfield-d-r-millers-1862-harvest-of-death/.
4. Roos, Dave. "How Many Were Killed on D-Day?", *History.com*, 5 Jun. 2019, https://www.history.com/news/d-day-casualties-deaths-allies.
5. Civil War Veterans' Card File, 1861-1866 Index.
6. "Prohibition Candidate for Governor of Kansas," *The Fulcrum, [Burlingame, Kansas]*, 10 Aug. 1900, p.1.
7. Frank Holsinger's letter, written on February 29, 1892, to John M. Gould courtesy of Tom Clemens.
8. Lewis Waltz photograph courtesy of *Historical Data Systems*; biographical information sourced from *Ancesry.com*.
9. Hopewell Veterans photograph courtesy of Barbara Sponsler Miller.
10. Holsinger, Frank. *War Talks in Kansas volume 1 - How does one Feel Under Fire*, F. Hudson Publishing Co., 1906, pp.298-300.
11. Holsinger letter to Gould, Feb. 29, 1892.
12. George V.A. Juda photograph courtesy of Ronn Palm; biographical information sourced from *Ancestry.com*.
13. James Cleaver photograph courtesy of the Bedford County Courthouse; biographical information sourced from *Ancestry.com*.

    "Minutes of the 97th Session of the Baltimore Annual Conference of the Methodist Episcopal Church," 9-15 Mar. 1881.

    "James Cleaver obituary," *Bedford Gazette*, 27 Jan. 1911, p.1.
14. Holsinger, Frank., "What it was to a Pennsylvanian and What he Saw of it." *The National Tribune*, 9 April 1908, p.7.
15. Official Army Record, #36, Col. Albert Magilton (8th PA Res).
16. Sypher, J.R. *History of the Pennsylvania Reserves*, Lancaster PA, Elias Barr & Co. 1865, p.386.
17. Official Army Record, volume 19-chapter 31, #28, Capt. James MacThomson (107th PA).
18. Dawes, Rufus. Antietam Cornfield Trail Guide–Stop 7, *National Park Service*, 12 August 2021, https://www.nps.gov/anti/planyourvisit/cornfield-trail-guide-stop-7.htm.
19. Thomas, Mary Warner and Sauers, Richard A., *The Civil War Letters of 1st Lt. James B. Thomas*, Butternut and Blue Publishers. 1995, p.97.
20. Frederick Frazey photograph courtesy of jeagle00 in *Ancestry.com*; biographical information sourced from *Ancestry.com*.
21. Locke, William Henry. *The Story of the Regiment*, Philadelphia, J.B. Lippincott & Co. 1868, p.126.
22. Gottfried, *Maps of Antietam*, p.136.
23. Locke, *The Story of the Regiment*, p.128.
24. Locke, *The Story of the Regiment*, pp.133-134.
25. Harsuff's Brigade battlefield marker on Cornfield Avenue.
26. Frances & Sarah Pee photographs courtesy of Niels Witkamp; biographical information sourced from *Ancestry.com*.
27. *History of the One hundred and twenty-fifth regiment, Pennsylvania volunteers,* 1862-1863, Lippincott, 1906, pp.32-34.
28. *History of the One hundred and twenty-fifth regiment*, pp.38-41, 50.

29. *History of the One hundred and twenty-fifth regiment*, p.62.
    Huyette, Miles C. *The Maryland Campaign and the Battle of Antietam*, Hammond Press, 1915, p.28.
30. Bosbyshell, Oliver C. and McCamant, Thomas. *Pennsylvania at Antietam,* Harrisburg Publishing Company, 1906, p.134.
31. *History of the One hundred and twenty-fifth regiment*, pp.63-66.
32. Huyette, *The Maryland Campaign*, p.35-36.
33. Bosbyshell, *Pennsylvania at Antietam*, p.137.
34. *Historical Data Systems* record and photograph. http://www.civilwardata.com/.
35. Huyette, *The Maryland Campaign*, p.38.
36. Huyette, *The Maryland Campaign*, p.36-37.
37. Official Army Record, volume 19, chapter 31, #172–Jacob Higgins (125th PA).
38. Higgins, Jacob. "At Antietam," *The National Tribune,* 3 June 1886, p.1.
39. Official Army Record, #172–Jacob Higgins.
40. Huyette, *The Maryland Campaign*, p.38-39.
41. Bosbyshell, *Pennsylvania at Antietam*, p.138.
42. Higgins. *The National Tribune*, 3 June 1886, p.1.
43. Official Army Record, # 172–Jacob Higgins.
44. Higgins. *The National Tribune*, 3 June 1886, p.2.
45. Higgins. *The National Tribune*, 3 June 1886, p.2.
46. *History of the One hundred and twenty-fifth regiment*, p.201.
47. *History of the One hundred and twenty-fifth regiment*, p.85.
48. Huyette, *The Maryland Campaign,* p.48.
49. Miles Huyette photograph courtesy of Frederick Kron.
50. Photograph courtesy of *Flickr*, https://www.flickr.com/photos/lcd1863/5925088031.
51. William and Anna Campbell photographs courtesy of Sondra Lucas; biographical information sourced from *Ancestry.com.*
52. David Harclerode photographs courtesy of Thomas McGuire; biographical information sourced from *Ancestry.com*.
53. *Biographical review containing life sketches of leading citizens of Somerset and Bedford counties*, Boston, MA, Biographical Review Pub. Co. 1899, p.99-100.
54. Jamison family information and photographs courtesy of Gaylord W. Little.
    History of the One hundred and twenty-fifth regiment, p.206.
55. "Eyewitness account of Antietam," *Shoppers Guide*, 25 January 2014, pg. 2; Ancestry.com.
56. Banks, John, "A visit to Widow Hoffman's farm at Antietam", *John Banks Civil War Blog,* 23 April 2018, https://john-banks.blogspot.com/2018/04/masterpiece-visit-to-widow-hoffmans.html.
57. "Funeral of Corporal John A. Kelly," *Altoona Tribune,* 2 October 1862, p.3.
58. William Malone biographical information from *Ancestry.com* and *Findagrave.com*.
59. "Major Holsinger Dies Suddenly," *Kansas City Sun,* 14 January 1916, p.3.
    David Long photograph courtesy of Alann Schmidt.

4. Harpers Ferry

Enlistment, casualty, and other individual soldier details were sourced from my first book, Civil War Soldiers of Bedford County Pennsylvania.

Many resources contributed to the regimental locations shown on the battlefield map of Harpers Ferry. These sources include the regimental history books, memoirs, and the following book.

Gottfried, Bradley M. The Maps of Antietam, Sevas Beatie, 2012.

1. John Lowery photograph and biographical information courtesy of Barbara Sponsler Miller, Carolyn Miller Carroll.
2. John Schetrompf photograph courtesy of Barbara Sponsler Miller; biographical information sourced from *Ancestry.com.*
3. Joseph B. Smith photograph courtesy of Debbie Crousern; biographical information sourced from

4. George W. Sponsler photograph and biographical information courtesy of Barbara Sponsler Miller, Carolyn Miller Carroll.
5. Gottfried, Bradley M. *The Maps of Antietam,* Savas Beatie, 2012, p.90.
6. Moore, Frank. *The Rebellion Record; a diary of American Events*, New York, G.P. Putnam, 1863, p.440.
7. Gottfried, *The Maps of Antietam*, pp.100-102.
8. Gottfried, *The Maps of Antietam*, p.104.
9. Mearkle, Kevin. *Civil War Soldiers of Bedford County*, 2021
10. Moore, Frank, *The Rebellion Record*, pp. 447-448
11. Sears, Stephen W. *Landscape Turned Red*, Ticknor & Fields, 1983, p.254.
12. Nathan P. R. Smith POW record courtesy of Pat Smith.

5. Gettysburg

Enlistment, casualty, and other individual soldier details were sourced from my first book, Civil War Soldiers of Bedford County Pennsylvania.

Many resources contributed to the regimental locations shown on the battlefield maps of Gettysburg. These sources include the regimental history books, memoirs, official army records, newspaper articles, and the following two books.

Gottfried, Bradley M. *The Maps of Gettysburg*, Sevas Beatie, 2007.

Laino, Philip. *Gettysburg Campaign Atlas,* Gettysburg Publishing LLC. 2015.

1. Augustyn, Adam. "Battle of Gettysburg," *Britannica,* https://www.britannica.com/event/Battle-of-Gettysburg.
   "10 Facts: Gettysburg." *American Battlefield Trust,* https://www.battlefields.org/learn/articles/10-facts-gettysburg.
2. Mearkle, Kevin, *Civil War Soldiers of Bedford County Pennsylvania*, Ingram-Spark, 2021.
   "Gordon's Brigade," *Stone Sentinels,*
   https://gettysburg.stonesentinels.com/confederate-headquarters/gordons-brigade/.
3. Locke, *The Story of the Regiment*, p.226.
   Official Army Report, volume 27 - chapter 39, #56 – Col. Chapman Biddle (142nd PA).
4. Official Army Report, volume 27 - chapter 39, #44 Col. Richard Coulter (11th PA).
5. Official Army Report, volume 27 - chapter 39, #56 – BG Thomas A Rowley (142nd PA).
   Official Army Report, #56 – Col. Chapman Biddle.
6. Uriah Sparks photograph courtesy of Jack & Carolyn Sparks; biographical information from *Ancestry.com*.
7. Joseph Armstrong photograph courtesy of Fort Bedford Museum; biographical information sourced from *Ancestry.com*.
8. Official Army Report, #44 Col. Coulter.
9. Locke, *The Story of the Regiment*, p.229.
10. Vautier, John D. *History of the 88th Pennsylvania Volunteers,* Philadelphia, J.B. Lippincott, p.135.
    Official Army Report, #44 Col. Coulter.
11. Gottfried. *The Maps of Gettysburg*, p.149.
12. Alfred Gracey photograph courtesy of Barbara Sponsler Miller; biographical information sourced from *Ancestry.com*.
13. George Gracey photograph courtesy of Stacychuck1 in *Ancestry.com*; biographical information sourced from *Ancestry.com*.
14. Laino. *Gettysburg Campaign Atlas,* p.127.
15. Official Army Report, #56 – Col. Chapman Biddle.
    Laino. *Gettysburg Campaign Atlas,* p.124.
16. Laino. *Gettysburg Campaign Atlas,* p.126.
17. Gottfried. *The Maps of Gettysburg*, p.183.
18. Thomas & Benjamin F Lohr photograph courtesy of Bedford Historical Society; biographical information sourced from *Ancestry.com*.
19. Locke, *The Story of the Regiment,* pp.231-232.
20. Hamilton, James. "The 110th Regiment in the Gettysburg Campaign," *Philadelphia Weekly Press,* 24 February 1896.

21. Heiser, John. "The Mears Party and the Medal of Honor, Part 1," *Blog of Gettysburg Nat'l Military Park,* 12 July 2018, https://npsgnmp.wordpress.com/2018/07/12/the-mears-party-and-the-medal-of-honor-part-1/
22. William W VanOrmer photograph courtesy of Ronn Palm; biographical information sourced from *Ancestry.com.*
23. Laino. *Gettysburg Campaign Atlas*, pp.219-234.
24. Hamilton, James. "The 110th Regiment Gettysburg Campaign."
25. DeTrobriand, Regis. *Four Years with the Army of the Potomac*, Boston, Ticknor and Co. 1889, p.497.
26. Hamilton, James. "The 110th Regiment Gettysburg Campaign."
27. Benjamin Shoemaker photograph courtesy of Sandra Breighne; biographical information sourced from *Ancestry.com.*
28. John I. Miller photograph courtesy of Bedford Historical Society; biographical information sourced from *Ancestry.com.*
29. John S. Border photograph courtesy of Squitchel in *Ancestry.com;* biographical information sourced from *Ancestry.com.*
30. Thomas G. Livingston photograph courtesy of Bedford Historical Society; biographical information sourced from *Ancestry.com.*
31. DeTrobriand. *Four Years with the Army of the Potomac*, pp.500-501.
32. White, Kristopher. "Battle of Gettysburg-The Wheatfield–quote from Pvt. Robert H. Carter, 22nd MA", *American History TV*, 2 July 2018, https://www.c-span.org/video/?447809-6/battle-gettysburg-wheatfield.
33. Nicholson, John P, et al. *Pennsylvania at Gettysburg: ceremonies at the dedication of the monuments*, W.S. Ray-State Printer, 1914, p.597.
34. William Nelson photographs courtesy of Stephanie Perry; biographical information sourced from *Ancestry.com.*
35. Americus Enfield photograph courtesy of JNicholson in *Findagrave.com*; biographical information sourced from *Ancestry.com.*
36. William and Ann Lowery photograph courtesy of Tony Klingensmith; biographical information sourced from *Ancestry.com.*
37. Benjamin F. Oliver photograph courtesy of *Harrisburg Telegraph* Obituary, 20 Jun. 1928; biographical information sourced from *Ancestry.com.*
38. William Raley Albright photograph courtesy of Bedford Historical Society; biographical information sourced from Jeff Whetstone and from *Ancestry.com.*

Photograph on the back cover of Bedford County Veterans at the Gettysburg National Cemetery courtesy of Aimee Stout Benitez.

www.ingramcontent.com/pod-product-compliance
Lightning Source LLC
Chambersburg PA
CBHW050805220426
43209CB00089BA/1714